BLOODAXE POETRY
INTRODUCTIONS: 2

Books by Neil Astley

ANTHOLOGIES

Staying Alive: real poems for unreal times
(Bloodaxe Books, 2002; Miramax Books, USA, 2003)
Pleased to See Me: 69 very sexy poems (Bloodaxe Books, 2002)
Do Not Go Gentle: poems for funerals (Bloodaxe Books, 2003)
Being Alive: the sequel to Staying Alive (Bloodaxe Books, 2004)
Passionfood: 100 Love Poems (Bloodaxe Books, 2005)

BLOODAXE POETRY INTRODUCTIONS

1: *Elizabeth Alexander, Moniza Alvi,*
Imtiaz Dharker, Jackie Kay (2006)
2: *Hans Magnus Enzensberger, Miroslav Holub,*
Marin Sorescu, Tomas Tranströmer (2006)
FURTHER TITLES TO BE ANNOUNCED

NOVELS

The End of My Tether (Flambard Press, 2002; Scribner, 2003)
The Sheep Who Changed the World (Flambard Press, 2005)

BLOODAXE POETRY INTRODUCTIONS

2

edited by
NEIL ASTLEY

BLOODAXE BOOKS

ISBN: 1 85224 739 8

First published 2006 by
Bloodaxe Books Ltd,
Highgreen,
Tarset,
Northumberland NE48 1RP.

www.bloodaxebooks.com
For further information about Bloodaxe titles
please visit our website or write to
the above address for a catalogue.

Bloodaxe Books Ltd acknowledges
the financial assistance of
Arts Council England, North East.

SPECIAL THANKS

To Alison Davis, especially, for thinking up this series,
and to Kennet Havgaard for his portraits used on the covers
(of people unconnected with the books or authors featured).

Cover printing by J. Thomson Colour Printers Ltd, Glasgow.

Printed in Great Britain by
Bell & Bain Limited, Glasgow, Scotland.

CONTENTS

TOMAS TRANSTRÖMER

HANS MAGNUS ENZENSBERGER

Hans Magnus Enzensberger is Germany's most important poet, as well as a provocative cultural essayist, a highly influential editor and one of Europe's leading political thinkers. His poetry's social and moral criticism of the post-war world owes much to Marxism, yet insists on the freedoms which have often been denied by Communist governments; like Orwell he maintains that satire and criticism should not be party-political.

Born in 1929 in the Bavarian town of Kaufbeuren, he grew up in Nazi Nuremberg. His father was a telecommunications engineer and his mother worked in a kindergarten. He studied German literature, philosophy and languages at the Universities of Elangen, Freiburg im Breisgau and Hamburg, and in Paris at the Sorbonne, completing his doctorate in 1955 with a thesis on the poetics of Clemens Brentano. At Freiburg the philosopher Martin Heidegger was an influential figure, but Enzensberger found him 'disagreeably authoritarian'. He then worked as a radio editor in Stuttgart until 1957.

Like all his books, his first collection, *defence of the wolves* (1957), provoked wildly differing reactions, with one reviewer calling his poetic critique of postwar Germany an 'unintentional parody of poetry', while another saw it as 'the first great political poetry since Brecht' from Germany's first 'angry young man'. He has always been a controversial figure in Germany, managing to upset even his admirers, but 'that's how it should be. It's a sign of vitality. I would be disappointed if there were a lukewarm, benevolent indifference.'

He was a founder member of Group 47, a loose grouping of disaffected German intellectuals including Heinrich Böll and Günter Grass, generally viewed as the most influential movement after the war, although Enzensberger now talks of the group as 'a historical myth': 'It just so happened that after the war there were a few guys who felt uneasy about the country, to put it mildly. It was like living with an enormous corpse in the cupboard.' Franz-Josef Strauss famously called them *Schmeissfliegen* (blowflies): writers whose attacks on its political institutions seemed to risk damaging Germany's clean postwar image.

In 1960 he published his pioneering anthology, *Museum der modernen Poesie* (Museum of modern poetry), introducing German readers to writers such as William Carlos Williams, Fernando Pessoa and Lars Gustafsson, but also expressing in his title his view that Modernism was defunct. In 1965 he founded the radical periodical *Kursbuch* (Railway Timetable), which published critical texts on the media and language and became a legendary forum for the student movement. In 1980 he founded the journal *Transatlantic*, and in 1985 began editing the prestigious book series Die Andere Bibliothek, now featuring nearly 250 titles, among them *The watermark of poetry, or The art and enjoyment of reading poems* (1985) by one Andreas Thalmayr. He used the same pseudonym for *Poetry gets on my nerves! First aid for stressed readers* (2004), a playfully ironic guide to the subject for younger readers in the spirit of his *Poetry Machine* installation (2000) – which caused something of a stir in Germany when he demonstrated how it could churn out lines of "poetry" at the touch of a button. 'Some of the poems are quite enjoyable,' he told a journalist. 'So I made a remark that was not well taken by some poets. I said anybody who can't do better than the machine should put away their pen.'

From 1961 he spent long periods abroad, living in Norway, Italy and the USA as well as West Berlin, before settling in Munich in 1979, where he still lives. He has also travelled to Mexico, South America, the Soviet Union, China and the Near East. A year in Cuba, in 1969 – where Castro denounced him as a CIA agent – inspired his master work, *The Sinking of the Titanic* (1978). He has translated poetry from English, French, Spanish, Italian, Swedish and Norwegian, and his own work has been translated into many languages. He has received numerous prizes and honours, including the Georg Büchner Prize (1963), Ernst Robert Curtius Prize (1997) and Heinrich Heine Prize (1998) in Germany, as well as Italy's Premio Bollati and the Spanish Premio Príncipe de Asturias.

Enzensberger's books include several on culture and politics which have been translated into English, among these *Europe, Europe*

(1989), *Mediocrity and Delusion* (1992) and *Civil War* (1994), as well as two bestselling works for young people, *The Number Devil* (1998), an entertaining look at maths, and *Where Were You, Robert?* (2000), about history. In 2004 *Dialoge zwischen Unsterblichen, Lebendigen und Toten* (Dialogues between immortals, the living and the dead) was published in Germany, a book of prose pieces on the influence of historical figures on the present-day *zeitgeist*.

His introduction to English readers came with a Penguin *Selected Poems* in 1968. His much larger, bilingual Bloodaxe *Selected Poems* of 1994 covers many collections published over 30 years, up to *Music of the Future* (1991), including *The Sinking of the Titanic*, which *The Guardian* called 'a brilliant fantasia on the foundering of western society'. For George Szirtes, writing in the *New Statesman*, it was 'a dramatic and philosophical statement of compulsive power …our emotions and our reason are driven along together as in the best of Brecht. We hear in Enzensberger the human voice amongst human voices, feel the extraordinariness of ordinary men.' Bloodaxe has also published two later collections, *Kiosk* (1995/1997) and *Lighter than Air: moral poems* (1999/2002). In Germany he recently published *Die Elixiere der Wissenschaft* (The Elixirs of Science, 2002), a gathering of his poetry and prose relating to science, followed by collection of 99 meditations, *Die Geschichte der Wolken* (The History of the Clouds, 2003).

SOME RESPONSES TO HANS MAGNUS ENZENSBERGER'S WORK:

'Hans Magnus Enzensberger is a poet of formidable intelligence and range. Like Brecht before him, he combines an intense political imagination with lyric gusto. The reader discovers in him both a satirist and a friend' – GEORGE STEINER.

'What Enzensberger (whose scepticism outpaced his Marxism) shares with Bertolt Brecht, his most obvious forebear, is less a common ideological commitment than the capacity to make poetry out of the plainest and most transparent language; to transform what, at first sight, might seem low-key laconic utterances into socially and politically resonant, even parabolic poems…Troubled by history, fascinated by politics, steeped in science, Enzensberger illuminates a path through the clutter of modern Western culture, wittily exposing the banality of its obsessions and the shallowness of its moral perspectives' – DENNIS O'DRISCOLL, *Times Literary Supplement*.

'From the first, Enzensberger's special function as a poet and prose writer arose from his awareness of being a West German just old enough to have received his early conditioning in the Third Reich, though he was only fifteen years old when it collapsed. Unlike many of his seniors and coevals, he was not content to blame the "wolves" of an older generation for what that order had perpetrated. If he was to be the conscience of his own generation, as he was widely acknowledged to be in the 60s and 70s, he had to break with the conformism and the "inwardness" – the moral alibi of so many of his predecessors – that had allowed the German "lambs" to feel good while going to the slaughter, their own as well as that of those classified as goats. As recently as in his latest prose book, *Aussichten auf den Bürgerkrieg* (Civil War) of 1993, Enzensberger insisted that the meekness of the lambs was and remains a prerequisite for every atrocity committed by the wolves. The peculiar tough-mindedness of his stance, always combined with the utmost elegance, is inseparable from that early recognition. [...]

Enzensberger's modernity – as distinct from modernism – lies in his exceptional grasp of the pluralism of our age. His work embodies the multiple awareness with which all of us are cursed by the sheer quantity and instant transmission of information, disaster, scandal, sensation, selected news of the world. It has been Enzensberger's distinction not to have recoiled from this battery of appeals to our interest, sympathy, anger and outrage, but to have gone out of his way to be more widely informed than most of the more specialised transmitters – about science and technology as much as the most diverse societies, their economics and politics, not to mention linguistics, history and the arts' – MICHAEL HAMBURGER, from his Introduction to *Selected Poems* (Bloodaxe Books, 1994).

PETER FORBES

Enzensberger: The Caged Poet

When Hans Magnus Enzensberger came to Brighton [1994] to launch his Bloodaxe *Selected Poems* and talk with Michael Ignatieff at the Festival of Literature, he spoke about his poems of the 1950s, the years of German reconstruction: 'I felt caged,' he said, 'by the historical situation, you see. I needed to get out of the German cage.'

Traps and cages recur in Enzensberger's work. Some of his best poems show people hopelessly in thrall to forces they can't understand, let alone control: the 33 year-old-woman, a child of '68, trapped by trendiness, a pair of spinsters imprisoned in their grey world of an ironmonger's shop. Enzensberger has a passion to probe such traps while reserving the right to fly off at a tangent occasionally.

10

He tells of the formative influence on him of 'The Story of Flying Robert' from *Struwelpeter*. In that story 'All good little girls and boys' are exhorted to 'stay at home and mind their toys', but not Robert, who thinks, 'No, when it pours it is better out of doors'. He is blown away in a storm with his red umbrella and never seen again. 'I remember well, when I was five years old, it had the opposite effect on me – I identified with him.' The story neatly encapsulates both Enzensberger's relish for getting into trouble by heading into the storm, and his desire to get 'anywhere out of this world'.

A slim, bright-eyed 64, who affects a Tom Wolfish line in clothes, Enzensberger is urbanity personified, and he gives the impression of having a great store of amusements laid up as an antidote to *Weltschmerz*. He spent his first night in Brighton on the Pier. He is a political heavyweight who has retained the light touch.

And he is no stranger to mischief: in 1969 he slipped the German cage to spend a year in Cuba – the result was denunciation by Castro as a CIA agent, Enzensberger's recognition that communism as it existed was no alternative to capitalism, and *The Sinking of the Titanic*, the long poem sequence that is widely regarded as his greatest poem. In this he achieves what he regards as essential for writing poetry: 'a certain distance from what you're talking about'. In *The Titanic* and his next collection *The Fury of Disappearance*, Enzensberger attains a miraculous balance between gravitas and a debonair, flyaway manner. He has always, like Louis MacNeice (a poet he resembles in several respects), valued the moment: 'one way of puncturing the excessive continuity of things in public life – even in private life – is of course the instant, the moment – this is something the mystics knew very well, that you could puncture the flow of time'.

But it is always reality he returns to; he deals curtly with the post-modern notion that the representation of reality, whether in science or art, is impossible: 'I'm rather impatient with all this talk about the disappearance of the subject, the I. It is a French fashion that has colonised the academic world. People at large are not affected by this.'

His poems are full of marvellously evoked paintings, especially Dutch and German landscapes and still lives, and it is above all the illusion of representation that grips him, the creation of this Janus object, part figment, part recreation of a version of reality. 'Before landscape painting there was in a certain sense no landscape,' he says. And what attracts him in still life is the link with science – the fact that many still-life artists were naturalists.

Enzensberger's breadth of interests seems inspired by the Enlight-enment tradition he has espoused. Politics enters his poetry auto-matically: 'As little as I could imagine poetry that excluded all things to do with love and sex, how could I exclude something which so much impinges on my life.' He is a most tenacious critic of Western civilisation, but he abhors the tendency of some commentators to speak as if they were outside the thing they criticise. He is the diagnostician who attempts to show us – himself included – just what we are up to.

His new prose book *Civil War* (Granta Books) locates the crisis firmly in the West, and not in Bosnia, the former Soviet Union or any other place we are currently wringing our hands about. Put simply, he believes that civil war is not something that happens elsewhere, it is now omnipresent. He calls the urban violence of the skinheads, racist gangs and crack dealers 'molecular civil war'. He believes that all perpetrators of contemporary mass violence are on par in that – unlike communism and fascism – they have no ideology behind them: 'Right-wing violence is not nationalistic. The classical nationalist was in some sense a nation builder, whereas these people are nation destroyers. A large part of public disclosure still insists on taking at face value the rationale handed out. In Yugoslavia the Serb nationalists might or might not have a cause: making Serbia an uninhabitable place.' He does not believe that Germany's problems with racist violence are any different from anyone else's: 'Most of the more terrifying aspects of the 90s are not specific German problems. The whole question of migration and xenophobia is all over Western Europe, even in countries where you would have thought it was out of the question, the Scandinavian countries.'

The three essays in *Civil War* look at xenophobia and the ruined Europe of 1945, out of which grew the order which collapsed in 1989 and has still to be resolved into a new pattern. He believes the common factor in all of the world's troubled societies is a collapse of patriarchy, a power vacuum. 'Civil war has existed for a very long time. Probably before the 18th century nobody expected that humanity would establish all over the world the rule of law. Huge expectations have been held for the past two and a half centuries. History has come back with a vengeance.'

This is not what anybody wants to hear, least of all the Germans, who, Enzensberger believes, have never quite recovered from the Thirty Years War of the 17th century. He has made a habit of telling Germans what they don't want to hear about reunification or Saddam Hussein. Now in suggesting that Germany (and the West) puts its house in order before tackling the globe's other trouble spots, he is flouting one of the most cherished pieties of the German liberal-left. He shares their feelings but believes that with 40 or more civil wars raging throughout the world, universal policing is now impossible.

Civil War shows Enzensberger's appetite for controversy undiminished, but while contemplating the world situation with alarm, his intellectual composure is unruffled. He speaks fondly of his his fine book publishing venture, Die Andere Bibliothek, of his collection of German and Dutch Old Masters, of typography and new poetry. At the public reading with Michael Ignatieff he lambasts the 'spooky makebelieve' of the Serbs in resurrecting spurious ancient justifications for their terror. Like Primo Levi, Enzensberger possesses in abundance the only possible antidote to encroaching madness and barbarity: an unshakeable faith in clear thinking, human decency, and the curious charm of the material world.

This article first appeared in *The Independent* (6 August 1994).

MICHAEL MARCH
In Conversation with Hans Magnus Enzensberger

MM: You've experienced the onset of the slaughter and destruction of Europe living in Nuremberg as a child. Tell us a little bit about your childhood experiences.

HME: Probably everybody is marked to some degree by their historical experiences and mine, of course, was growing up in Nazi Germany, during the Second World War, the aftermath of the war. I was a child at the end of the war, I was 17, and that leaves a sort of indelible mark. Though I do not envy the young people who grew up in postwar times, in times of economic well-being, because this kind of experience gives you a background, some dimension, which is inexplicable.

MM: Is that why you became a poet?

HME: It's very hard to say how you become a poet. It's probably something to do with language first of all, the kind of thing which reverberates in your head. You develop a taste for phrases, for metaphors, for verse, for rhythm, and so on. It's a natural process, it's not an ambition, you don't plan to be a poet. In some respects it's a vice, like an alcoholic who starts drinking. He doesn't quite realise what it means, what it implies, he just starts to have a drink, and so you start to write a verse or a few verses and after a while you discover that you cannot very well leave it alone. So it is more than a habit, certainly. I couldn't leave it alone, that's all.

MM: Do you see your poems as political poems?

HME: You see, I dislike the notion of the poet as specialist. In the 19th century there used to be the idea that the poet is a specialist in emotion, in feelings, in sentimentality, in nature. And then there's the specialist in politics, who is a socially engaged poet – the man who is on the tribune, talking to the masses. I personally don't like these specialisations. A poet is an omnivore. I don't want to be a specialist.

MM: As a distinguished editor, which of the post-war poets do you find important for yourself?

HME: I wouldn't like to make a hit-list, because the habit of making lists is a bit presumptuous. I was never an avant-garde poet, though I respect the historical avant-garde of 1910. The poets who are important for me are a very mixed lot: Catullus, for example, John Donne, and César Vallejo. I always pick something up when I can use it. In some sense, artists and poets are egoists because their criterion is not what is objectively good or important, but what is useful.

MM: How do you view the world after Germany's most recent defeat?

HME: When I was 17 or 18, Germans were the pariahs of the world. You could hardly go abroad, you did not have a passport, you were, morally speaking, an object of contempt. A German was the bad guy. And I don't know how it came about, but certainly the Germans had a lot of historical luck, because the peace which was made between the Western allies and the Germans was a very intelligent peace, unlike Versailles after the First World War. But of course, we didn't have the good heart of the allies to thank, we had the Russians to thank. Because of the Russians West Germany was put on its feet again, for strategic reasons. Still, it was a very remarkable and far-sighted peace which we were granted. The Western allies virtually forced democracy upon us. The real sensation is that it worked. Germany became an inhabitable place, and to that extent it was a success story. Now of course, this story is at its end.

MM: The miracle has moved east, with the impending imposition of democracy in Iraq and the Arab world.

HME: Yes, under much more difficult circumstances. Nobody knows how this is going to work out, and it's also a question whether you can apply the same pattern to all sorts of civilisations. At this point I would like to include a list of all the things that I am not: I'm not a sociologist, I'm not a political scientist, I'm not a philosopher, I'm not a prophet, I'm not a futurologist.

MM: But you knew enough to support the ousting of Saddam Hussein.

Why has this caused such a furore in Germany?

HME: I'm not quite sure about the reasons, but there is, of course, a pacifist tradition in Western Germany due to two world wars, when the Germans were roundly beaten, perhaps for their own good. The military does not have a high standing in society. That's part of the explanation. Another part is our relationship to the United States which is very complicated, very ambiguous, ambivalent you might say. There is sympathy, but there is also dislike for America in the world.

As for for myself, I have one overriding political passion – my hatred of dictators. Dictators are the worst criminals in the world. I rejoice in the downfall of any dictator. This is a visceral reaction. It's a wonderful moment to see a statue of Stalin crushing down! A moment of real joy. Still, all things being said, I am not a defender of American foreign policy, nor am I claiming that the United States should not obey the rules of international law, and I'm not saying that the lies which were involved in this operation by Mr Bush were not lies. The only thing I maintain is that if a bastard like Saddam Hussein disappears it's all to the good. That's all I'm saying.

MM: It's a personal joy.

HME: Yes, it's a personal joy, but it's also based on experience. I would not be alive if the Allies had not made an end to Hitler.

MM: Why?

HME: I would not have been tolerated. I would have been done away with.

MM: Are we not drifting back to Joseph Roth's time, to the fall of empires, to the disintegration of Europe?

HME: The old empires were territorial empires. This is a new kind of empire, the American Empire. They don't need to annex places, they don't have colonies. They annex the economy, while remaining isolationists. Sometimes I feel sorry for the Americans, because to be number one is not a blessing. Whatever you do is wrong. When you intervene, you are an imperialist, when you don't intervene, as in Rwanda, then you are not doing your job. I'm happy we're not a great power in Europe, it's much better. Who wants to be number one? The Germans have tried once and failed! No, thank you very much.

Extract from a discussion at Prague Writers' Festival in March 2004. For the full text, go to http://www.pwf.cz

The End of Owls

I do not speak of what's yours,
I speak of the end of the owls.
I speak of turbot and whale
in their glimmering house,
in the sevenfold sea,
of the glaciers –
too soon they will calve –
raven and dove, the feathered witnesses,
of all that lives in the winds
and woods, and the lichen on rock,
of impassable tracts and the grey moors
and the empty mountain ranges:

Shining on radar screens
for the last time, recorded,
checked out on consoles, fingered
by aerials fatally Florida's marshes
and the Siberian ice, animal,
reed and slate all strangled
by interlinked warnings, encircled
by the last manoeuvres, guileless
under hovering cones of fire,
while the time-fuses tick.

As for us, we're forgotten.
Don't give a thought to the orphans,
expunge from your minds
your gilt-edged security feelings
and fame and the stainless psalms.
I don't speak of you any more,
planners of vanishing actions,
nor of me, nor of anyone.
I speak of that without speech,
of the unspeaking witnesses,
of otters and seals,
of the ancient owls of the earth.

[1960] MH

For the Grave of a Peace-loving Man

This one was no philanthropist,
avoided meetings, stadiums, the large stores.
Did not eat the flesh of his own kind.

Violence walked the streets,
smiling, not naked.
But there were screams in the sky.

People's faces were not very clear.
They seemed to be battered
even before the blow had struck home.

One thing for which he fought all his life,
with words, tooth and claw, grimly,
cunningly, off his own bat:

the thing which he called his peace,
now that he's got it, there is no longer a mouth
over his bones, to taste it with.

[1964] MH

Middle Class Blues

We can't complain.
We're not out of work.
We don't go hungry.
We eat.

The grass grows,
the social product,
the fingernail,
the past.

The streets are empty.
The deals are closed.
The sirens are silent.
All that will pass.

The dead have made their wills.
The rain's become a drizzle.
The war's not yet been declared.
There's no hurry for that.

We eat the grass.
We eat the social product.
We eat the fingernails.
We eat the past.

We have nothing to conceal.
We have nothing to miss.
We have have nothing to say.
We have.

The watch has been wound up.
The bills have been paid.
The washing-up has been done.
The last bus is passing by.

It is empty.

We can't complain.

What are we waiting for?

[1964] MH

Concert of Wishes

Sanad says: Give me my daily pita
Fräulein Brockmann looks for a comfortable little flat not too ex-
      pensive with a cooking recess and a broom cupboard
Véronique longs for world revolution
Dr Luhmann desperately needs to sleep with his mum
Uwe Köpke dreams of a perfect specimen of Thurn and Taxis seven
      silbergroschen pale blue imperforated
Simone knows exactly what she wants: to be famous Simply famous
      no matter what for or at what price
If Konrad had his way he'd simply lie in bed for ever
Mrs Woods would like to be tied up and raped quite regularly but
      only from behind and by a gentleman

18

Guido Ronconi's only desire is the unio mystica
Fred Podritzke would love to work over all those crackpot lefties with
    a length of gas piping until not one of them so much as twitches
If someone doesn't give him his steak and chips this minute Karel
    will blow his top
What Buck needs is a flash and nothing else

And peace on earth and a ham sandwich and the uncensored dia-
logue and a baby and a million free of tax and a moaning that
gives way to the familiar little breathless shrieks and a plush
poodle and freedom for all and off with his head and that the
hair we have lost will grow again overnight

[1971] MH

The Reprieve

Watching the famous eruption of a volcano on Heimaey, Iceland,
which was broadcast live by any number of TV teams,
I saw an elderly man in braces showered by sulphur and brimstone,
ignoring the storm, the heat, the video cables, the ash
and the spectators (including myself, crouching on my carpet
in front of the livid screen), who held a garden hose,
slender but clearly visible, aimed at the roaring lava,
until neighbours joined him, soldiers, children, firemen,
pointing more and more hoses at the advancing fiery lava
and turning it into a towering wall, higher and higher,
of lava, hard, cold and wet, the colour of ash, and thus postponing,
not forever perhaps, but for the time being at least,
the Decline of Western Civilisation, which is why
the people of Heimaey, unless they have died since,
continue to dwell unmolested by cameras
in their dapper white wooden houses,
calmly watering in the afternoon
the lettuce in their gardens, which, thanks to the blackened soil,
has grown simply enormous, and for the time being at least,
fails to show any signs of impending disaster.

[1978] HME

Vending Machine

He puts four dimes into the slot
he gets himself some cigarettes

He gets cancer
he gets apartheid
he gets a couple of far-away massacres

He gets more and more
for his four dimes
but for a moment all the things disappear

Even the cigarettes

He looks at the vending machine
He sees himself
For a fleeting moment
he almost looks like a man

Then very soon he is gone again
with a little click
there are his cigarettes

He has disappeared
it was just a fleeting moment
some kind of sudden bliss

He has disappeared
he is gone
buried under all the stuff he got
for his four dimes

[1980] MH

Clothes

Here they lie, still and cat-like
in the sun, in the afternoon,
your clothes, baggy,

undreaming, as if by chance.
They smell of you, faintly,
they almost take after you,
give away your dirt,
your bad habits,
the trace of your elbows.
They take their time, don't breathe,
are left over, limp, full of buttons,
properties, stains.
In the hands of a policeman,
a dressmaker, an archaeologist
they would reveal their seams,
their idle secrets. But where you are,
whether you suffer, what
you had always wanted to tell me
and never did, whether
what happened has happened
for love's sake or from need
or from negligence, and why
all this has come about as it did
when it was a question
of saving our skin,
whether you are dead by now
or have gone to wash your hair,
they do not tell.

[1980] MH

Visiting Ingres

Today he'd be painting for the Central Committee, or Paramount,
it all depends. But at that time a gangster still sweated
under his ermine, and the con-men had themselves crowned.
So let's have them, the insignia, pearls, the peacock feathers.

We find the artist pensive. He has stuffed himself
with 'choice ideas and noble passions'.
A laborious business. Expensive small armchairs, First or Second
        Empire,
it all depends. Soft chin, soft hands, 'Hellas in his soul'.

For sixty years this cold greed, every inch a craftsman,
till he's achieved it: fame, the rosette in his buttonhole.

These women, writhing in front of him on the marble
like seals made of risen dough: between thumb and forefinger
the breasts measured, the surface studied like plush,
tulle, glossy taffeta, the moisture in the corner of their eyes
glazed twelve times over like gelatine, the flesh colour smooth
and narcotic, better than Kodak: exhibited
in the École des Beaux-Arts, a venal eternity.

What's it all for? What for the tin of his decorations,
the fanatical industry, the gilt plaster eagles?

Curiously bloated he looks at eighty,
worn out, with that top hat in his left hand.
'It was all for nothing'. How can you say that, most honoured Maître!
What will the frame-maker think of you, the glazier?
your faithful cook, the undertaker? His only answer:

A sigh. Far above the clouds, oniric, the fingers of Thetis
that squirm like worms on Jupiter's black beard.
Reluctantly we take a last brief look
at the artist – how short his legs are! –
and tiptoe out of the studio.

[1980] MH

Old Revolution

A beetle lying on its back.
The old bloodspots are still on show
in the museum. Decades playing dead.
A sour smell from the mouth of thirty ministries.
At the Hotel Nacional four deceased musicians
are playing night by night the tango from '59:
Quizás, quizás, quizás.

By the murmur of a tropical rosary
History is taking a nap. Only those

who long for toothpaste, light bulbs
and spaghetti are tossing sleeplessly
between the damp bedsheets.

A sleepwalker in front of ten microphones
is preaching to his tired island:
After me nothing will follow.
It is finished.
The machine-guns glisten with oil.
The shirts are sticky with cane-juice.
The prostate has had it.

Wistfully the aged warrior
scans the horizon for an aggressor.
There is no one in sight. Even the enemy
has forgotten about him.

[1991] MH

Humble-bee, Bumble-bee

Amazing, how she takes off
quivering with energy,
how she rises
and, softly thudding,
hurls herself towards light
against the window-pane.

After the crash,
another attempt,
more practised in the approach,
more caution, less vehemence.
To freedom, to the sun.
The glass remains impenetrable.

The antennae more and more limp,
hopeless sallies.
The fall mere routine.
A life for art's sake.

Till she just lies there,
faintly twitching,
on the window-sill,
that furry singer.

[1995] MH

Presumption of Innocence

This seven-year-old girl on her trampoline,
how effortlessly, with her hair flying,
she gets the better of gravity;

the chef who, intent, the wooden spoon in his mouth,
licks, listens, waits for the flavour
behind the flavour to flow through his nostrils;

the hopelessly neglected tone-setter,
how with monkey-like relish
he hammers his cadenza into the keys;

the absent-minded couple in the midst of
syringes and beer cans on their clammy park bench
encased in each other;

the murderer who, beside himself with delight
at the ideal penalty-kick, forgets
his mission, his alibi, the place of the crime;

or the fat old woman over there who, blinking,
scratches herself, and ecstatically
plays with her sandy toes;

and the bent shoe-shine man, how he basks
in the reflection of the radiance which his saliva
has bewitched the leather toe-cap to yield:

these beings happy to the point of unconsciousness –
for a moment it isn't their fault
that they're no ordinary animals.

[1995] MH

Optimistic Little Poem

Now and then it happens
that somebody shouts for help
and somebody else jumps in at once
and absolutely gratis.

Here in the thick of the grossest capitalism
round the corner comes the shining fire brigade
and extinguishes, or suddenly
there's silver in the beggar's hat.

Mornings the streets are full
of people hurrying here and there without
daggers in their hands, quite equably
after milk or radishes.

As though in a time of deepest peace.

A splendid sight.

[1999] DC

Explaining the Declaration

It starts in the pub, in the back room
where seven drunks are gathered together,
war; it smoulders
in the crèche; the Academy
of Sciences hatches it;
no, in a delivery room in Gori
or Braunau it flourishes, on the net,
in the mosque; it sweats
from the small brain of the patriotic poet;
because someone is offended, because someone
has tasted blood, in God's name,
war rages, on grounds of colour,
in the bunker, for a joke, or by mistake;
because there have to be sacrifices

25

to save mankind, and these
especially at night, because of the oilfields;
for this, that even self-mutilation
has its attractions and because there's money
war starts, in a delirium
because of a football match;
for no such thing, for heaven's sake; yes, then;
though nobody wanted it; aha;
just like that, for pleasure, heroically
and because we can't think of anything better to do.

[1999] DC

World Market

What we need now is a sander,
a trimmer head, an interface card
flown in from Japan. Suddenly
there are souvenirs from Timbuktu,
icons, kidnapped babies. Everywhere
the same razorblades, the same
people at conferences and killer bees.
Car bombs do the rounds, wives
land from the catalogues,
bank accounts shift by satellite.
Brand new viruses come floating in.
Only now and then by the roadside
there's a beggar lying, motionless.

[1999] DC

Poor Cassandra

She was the only one who saw it coming,
just her: all this, she said,
will end badly. Of course
not a soul believed her.

A long long time ago. Now
everyone is saying it. Look
at the share index, the traffic jams
and the late-night news. The only question is
what 'all this' means, and *when?*
Till then of course
not a soul believes what everyone is saying.
Look at the second cars,
the beer gardens and the marriage announcements.

[1999] DC

Of His Own Free Will

'I love tea roses,' so you say, my friend,
'but a fat loss carried forward
is no bad thing either.'
'I could do with a vibrator,'
says your wife, 'and you give me
a first edition of Nietzsche.'

You hear it all the time.
But not everyone has, as you do,
comrade, the torment of choosing
between a case of Lafite
and a holiday on the Seychelles.
Not so easy, having free will.

Buridan's ass died of hunger.
Too much hay won't necessarily
make you a happy man, chum.
Between bolshevism and golf,
dollar and yen, Nike and Adidas
torn hither and thither, colleague

you're a reed in the wind. Come now,
sportsman, what shall it be?
Drive into a tree
in your BMW
or without more ado
OD? My dear chap

these are decisions
almost too weighty to take.
Play pendulum
ask your analyst
study the tea-leaves, and so
find out what you want.

[1999] DC

Should the Occasion Arise

Choose among the errors
given to you
but choose right.
Might it not be wrong
to do the right thing
at the wrong moment
or right
to do the wrong
at the right moment?
One false step
never to be made good.
The right error
should you miss it
may never come again.

[1999] DC

Enzensberger translators: [DC] David Constantine. [HME] Hans Magnus Enzensberger. [MH] Michael Hamburger. Pedants should note that what might appear to be errors in Enzensberger's self-translations are deliberate changes from the original German, his choice on occasions being to continue writing the poem in English when producing his English versions.

Dates: Year of first publication of original poem in book form in German.

MIROSLAV HOLUB

Miroslav Holub (1923-98) was the Czech Republic's foremost modern poet and one of her leading immunologists. His fantastical and witty poems give a scientist's bemused view of human folly and other life on the planet. Mixing myth, history and folktale with science and philosophy, his plainly written, sceptical poems are surreal mini-dramas often pivoting on paradoxes.

One of his translators, Ian Milner, has described the ironic and satiric impact and vivid appeal for Czech readers of Holub's early poems: 'Written against the background of the Stalinist 1950s and a rigorous censorship apparatus, the irony had to be expressed mostly by the indirect means of allegory and fable. Holub made himself a master of poetic double-talk enlivened by a mordant wit.' Another translator, Ewald Osers, recalls how the Czech authorities 'always had an uneasy feeling that in his surrealist way Holub might be poking fun at them. When in one of his poems he spoke of "a crowd of dwarves [applauding] in the king's palace", he was, somewhat to his surprise, summoned to the censor's office. It turned out that many of the members of the Communist Party Central Committee were rather short and that the passage would therefore have to be changed.'

Ted Hughes called Holub 'one of the half dozen most important poets writing anywhere', and his blackly comic poetry was one of several European influences on Hughes's *Crow*. According to Andrew Motion, 'Holub appealed to Hughes because his poetry encouraged a new kind of imaginative freedom, and partly because his subjects included the great European political and humanitarian crises of the mid-century'.

Miroslav Holub was born and grew up in Plzen (Pilsen), a heavily industrialised town in western Bohemia, Czechoslovakia. His father was a lawyer for the railways, his mother a high school teacher of French and German. He attended a gymnasium specialising in Greek and Latin, so that Homer and Virgil were the first poets he read carefully, while his mother shared with him her love of Goethe, Romain Rolland and French poetry. In 1942 he was conscripted to work on the railways. After the war he studied medicine at Charles University in Prague. He did not write poetry at all until the age of 30, when he started clinical research in pathology at a Prague hospital. In 1954 he joined the Institute of Biology (later Microbiology) at the Czechoslovak Academy of Sciences, and edited a popular scientific journal *Vesmír* (The Universe) until 1965. As a scientist, from the 1950s, he worked primarily in immunology, publishing over 150 articles in that area. His favoured laboratory animal was a hairless or "nude" mouse, a mutation which lacked a functioning thymus and so was unable to control its immune system. His many scientific publications include the monograph *Immunology of Nude Mice* (CRC Press, Boca Raton, Florida, 1989), and his essays on science and culture were collected in *The Dimension of the Present Moment* (Faber & Faber, 1990) and *Shedding Life: Disease, Politics and Other Human Conditions* (Milkweed Editions, MN, 1997).

Like the metaphysical English poet John Donne, Holub believed that poetry could be enriched by science, commenting on many occasions that he saw no conflict between his two fields. 'I have a single goal but two ways to reach it,' he said. 'I never switch them – I apply them both in turn. Poetry and science form the basis of my experience.' For him, scientific method and writing poetry were similar: 'The emotional, aesthetic and existential value is the same...when looking into the microscope and seeing the expected (or at times the unexpected, but meaningful) and when looking at the nascent organism of the poem.'

Interviewed by Dennis O'Driscoll on Irish television, he said: 'In science, we think in metaphors; when writing poems, I do an experiment all the time with a possible "yes" or "no" answer. The great difference comes when writing the "discussion", when you go for non-ambivalent words or just signs or symbols of something. The happiest science is, like theoretical physics, a science which doesn't need words. And, in poetry, you go for the most ambivalence, for the most meaning of a word or word structure.'

Holub's early poems appeared in Czech journals, but the Communist coup of February 1948 forced silence on all writers not approved by the Party; in the slightly more liberal climate of the late 1950s, he became active again, publishing his first collection at the age of 35 in 1958. His main literary influences by then were anti-lyrical and existentialist writers, Vítezslav Nezval and the Czech avant-garde, along with the French Surrealists (notably Jacques Prévert) and Italian cinematic neo-realism, and he was one of several young Czech writers who formed a group called Poetry of Everyday. In an article published in 1956, he criticised the ideological verse of the the Stalinist period, arguing that poetry needed to address ordinary life: 'Only by capturing life around us we may be able to express its dynamicism, the immense developments, rolling on around us and within us.' This meant giving up regular, rhymed, musical poetry, and writing free verse. By concentrating on what "things" mean, the poetry came not through lyricism but in the illumination. His poem 'In the microscope', published in his first collection, clearly shows what he meant by this.

As new poetry from outside Czechoslovakia started filtering in, Holub was inspired by the younger generation of Polish writers, especially Zbigniew Herbert, as well as by Germany's Hans Magnus Enzensberger and Günter Kunert, by Vasko Popa from Yugoslavia, and by American modernist poets, including the 'Beats' (Lawrence Ferlinghetti in particular) and William Carlos Williams. Evolving his own style in response to such disparate influences – and striving for 'something more concrete, beyond the personal' – his early progress was tentative, almost experimental: 'My coming into poetry was to find out if it was poetry, if what I was doing was poetry at all! I didn't find any correspondences, I just discovered I might be another kind...There are many types of poets and many types of poetry, just as there are different types of dogs.'

In 1963, Holub wrote: 'I prefer to write for people untouched by poetry...I would like them to read poems in such a matter-of-fact manner as when they are reading the newspaper or go to football matches. I would like people not to regard poetry as something more difficult, more effeminate or more praiseworthy.'

Because he had been active in the reformist movement – not as a dissident but as a liberal-minded cultural essayist – he was sacked from the Microbiological Institute in 1970. However, working his way up from a junior position at the Institute for Clinical and Experimental Medicine, he was allowed to continue his immunological research, but prevented for over ten years from publishing his literary work in Czechoslovakia, although translations of his poetry appeared throughout the 1970s in English and 37 other languages. Always refusing to join the official Writers' Union, he was a non-approved writer and as such could not publish a book; he then became a 'non-person' after his name had appeared on a government list, 'not for a poem, not for a book' but for signing a petition in the street.

When, during a period of thaw, his first book of Czech poetry for ten years appeared in 1982, it sold out in a day but could not be republished 'due to the paper shortage'. Discussing problems of translation with fellow writers, Holub used to claim, perhaps only half-jokingly, that he deliberately wrote his poems in a plain style in order that they *could be* translated, because none of his readers knew Czech. His Czech readers, however, were aware that he was still writing, recognising the style of a wittily idiosyncratic magazine column signed with his initials; he published these "essaylets" in book form in 1987 as *The Jingle Bell Principle* (an English translation by James Naughton was published by Bloodaxe in 1992).

Holub was first introduced to English readers in 1967 when Penguin published his *Selected Poems* in their Modern European Poets series. *Although* followed in 1971, and *Notes of a Clay Pigeon* – 'holub' meaning 'pigeon' in Czech – in 1977. In 1984 Bloodaxe published a selection of his more dramatic and complicated poetry from the 1970s and 1980s, *On the Contrary and other poems*, including the ill-fated 1982 collection as well as *Interferon, or On Theatre*, not published in Czechoslovakia until 1986, although parts of it were read or performed on stage in 1984 at Prague's Viola Poetry Theatre. Three years later, he was allowed to reprint the English translations of his poems from the 1950s and 1960s in *The Fly* (1987).

In 1989, he collected all the poems from *The Fly* and *On the Contrary*, plus additional work, in *Poems Before & After: Collected English Translations*. Less controversial by the time the book appeared in 1990, Holub's title was provocative in the Czech context with its implied reference to 1968. It was to have been published in this form in 1984, but the Czech authorities would not allow Holub to publish a Collected Poems in Britain or Czechoslovakia. He was not a member of the Writers' Union, and a Collected Poems was an honour reserved for only their most distinguished writers. The book was therefore published in two halves: the second half first in 1984, and the first half second in 1987. In 2006 an expanded edition was published including poems from his later collections, *Vanishing Lung Syndrome* (1990), *Supposed to Fly* (1996) and *The Rampage* (1997).

'A laying bare of things, not so much the skull beneath the skin, more the brain beneath the skull; the shape of relationships, politics, history; the rhythms of affections and disaffection; the ebb and flow of faith, hope, violence, art' – SEAMUS HEANEY.

'Witty, austere, classical, totally without egotism or sentimentality, he was a tireless wakener of the cynical and the servile. Throughout his poems and his prose writings, he insists that we can learn a humility that can oppose the corrupt and vicious totalitarian state – the labyrinth in which his favourite symbol the minotaur stalks and stumbles and growls. His poems have a strict, undogmatic openness and throwaway severity' – TOM PAULIN.

from Two Interviews with Miroslav Holub
by DENNIS O'DRISCOLL

1. DUBLIN, OCTOBER 1984

D'OD: How did your career as a poet begin?

MH: I started to write poems in the teens, as everybody does, in the romantic period. Then, later on, there was only one style acceptable in my country and I didn't use that style. I remember trying to get out a first volume of poems through a number of editors who just said 'Well, Mr Holub, it's not yet the proper thing'. Finally, I encountered a young editor, Jan Grossman, who asked me 'what is your style' and to make a selection of my work and present it to him. He established what I call now my way of writing poetry. This shows that what in theory we may call the personal style is not really that personal.

D'OD: What stirred you from experimenting in science to experimenting with words?

MH: Actually, I started both simultaneously. When I got my MD, it was about the time I finished something I regarded as a poetic text ripe for publication.

D'OD: I know you are tired of questions about the relationship of science to literature. Could I ask, though, whether you think you would have written substantially different poems had you been, say, a butcher or a teacher?

MH: Yes, very different. I am quite sure that science has had a decisive role in my life, especially at some times of life and of historical events. With science and the scientific affiliation, you are on a safe ground; and, whatever you do in the laboratory, you feel you are working on something very definite, very concrete. If I didn't have science, I would be left in a neurotic situation, with all my realisations, all my aspirations, all my hopes only in the word. Now I don't feel I am divided. I endorse myself by the scientific position in my poetic outlook.

D'OD: And you bring an analytical approach to your poetry, which is a scientific attitude.

MH: This was my intellectual aspiration – to bring the hard-centred approach of science into poetic thinking. I never wanted to write something which would be labelled a scientific poetry. I think it is a nonsense. I don't think it makes any sense to bring incomprehensibly scientific terms and words into poetic lines.

D'OD: Do you consider that someone reading the new work in *On the Contrary* is coming to a different, more complex poet than the one encountered in the 1967 Penguin *Selected Poems*?

MH: All my life, since the first book, I felt very strongly that the poetic profession means a permanent struggle between the will, between myself, and change. In all my books […] there is a fight between what I have established as my style – or what Mr Grossman has established as my style – and the attempt to change it. In the first volumes, I was condensed, expressed myself very shortly and was rather optimistic. In the latest volumes, I write longer poems in an attempt to write differently. I wouldn't say I have more complex meanings. Maybe I use more metaphors or images or surrealistic images and, above all, maybe I am less optimistic. That may not be connected with general conditions of life in Czechoslovakia or elsewhere. It may be just my growing older and, hopefully, wiser.

D'OD: How much of your work is lost in translation? I wouldn't say something has been lost.

MH: With almost all of my translators, we worked together. I had my say in the final version and, to me, it was very satisfactory. At times, I felt they were better in some translations, maybe in English, than in the Czech originals. Of course, with my first poems, which had a strict metre and rhyme, the English version is missing something.

D'OD: Do you harbour any doubts about poetry and how it relates to the world we live in?

MH: If I didn't have my laboratory work, I would be frustrated by the little influence that – I wouldn't exactly say poetry – whatever you call human intelligence and human inspiration has in the management of human affairs. I would feel desperate. But, with science, which would be applied directly or indirectly to the human condition, I don't feel this frustration.

D'OD: What exactly does your laboratory work consist of?

MH: I am engaged in the basic research in immunology, albeit I work in a hospital and we prepare some sera for the control of the rejection crisis for kidney-transplanted patients. My research is connected with the function of the thymus gland in experimental models. I have my model of nude mice, a mutation which lacks the thymus and therefore lacks the control of the immune system. Sometimes my work has a very poetic heading like 'Looking for a Thymus in a Thymusless Mouse'.

My main work comes from the optimistic 60s when I discovered, as part of a collective project, that the lymphocyte is the key cell of the whole immune system, the bearer of the inner wisdom of the body, that it knows about the antigenic properties of the outer world beforehand, that it leads your immune response to all intruders.*

D'OD: Is all of your poetry written after your day's work at the laboratory?

MH: Yes, strictly after work because you can't stay in science without giving it the proper time. […] Besides, in Czechoslovakia nowadays, I am not so much asked to write poems as I am encouraged to write scientific essays and this is very time-consuming. You may finish one poem (at least in my way of writing, because I have preconceived a poem one month ahead) by just writing it in half an hour. With an essay, it takes you hours.

D'OD: So you don't go through laborious drafts to reach the completed poem?

MH: No, no, never. I go through the drafts in my mind first. I have to know the skeleton of the poem. When I am almost sure of the result of the poem, I can sit down and try to write it – which is the oscillating process where the hazards and the freedom of expression come in. I can choose the words and the free associations occur (or usually don't occur, of course!). In the end, I see the poem and at times it may be even satisfactory – at least for the first evening, if not for the second one! Many times in the last year, it simply hasn't been satisfactory; but in my style, in my way, I can't correct it. I can correct it in my head beforehand; but I can't change it on the paper.

35

D'OD: An equally spontaneous poet with whom you have been compared is William Carlos Williams. Has he really had an influence on your poems?

MH: It is an influence in terms of encouragement: William Carlos Williams was a revelation for me above all as the poet of these condensed, heavy lines and as a physician, as a paediatrician, and I was reassured by his poems. But he didn't influence me in the way Jacques Prévert did. Prévert was somebody I tried to imitate and I succeeded in many places to the extent that I tried to write 'after Jacques Prévert'.

D'OD: One striking way in which you differ from those poets is in the degree to which you employ mythology, especially Greek mythology, in your verse. How do you reconcile this with your position as a modern poet noted for a scientific approach to writing?

MH: All poetry starts with lots of personal contradictions. My contradictions are, hopefully, not emotional but intellectual. I want to be very up-to-date, to be from this world of the second or third industrial revolution and of the first or second informational revolution. But still I have a classical education. I am one of the few who still had Greek in school; and it was a very good education, I must say. I was influenced both by the language, by the ancient Greek, and of course by all the tales, all the stories. For the feeling of contraposition with my very up-to-date aims, I use the old myths as a conflicting item in the poem. [...]

D'OD: You tend to keep yourself out of your poems, seldom allowing them to be directly autobiographical.

MH: Yes, there is a definite reason for that. I am not sure about my emotions or that I can write in a controlled way, which is my way, when under pressure of emotion. In general, I would say that one of the illnesses of modern poetry is too much subjectivity, too much toothache. I would say that we shouldn't be preoccupied, as poets, with ourselves.

Extract from 1984 interview first published in *Poetry Review* (October 1985).
*The asterisked paragraph is transplanted from the second interview below.

2. DALKEY, APRIL 1990

D'OD: Your poem, 'Homer', does not suggest that you relish the idea of a poet – revealing much about his private life.

MH: This was first induced by conditions where you could not tell the whole truth and you would prefer to show your abstention from the text. You are saying as much as you can but a part is missing and you too are missing. You are mimicking the intellectual situation.

Secondly, I don't like it at all – even now. This may be an attitude derived from the scientific habits. When you give a scientific lecture or make a scientific paper, there is no personal background given: no age, no numbers of girlfriends or wives or children. Nothing. So why should it be analysed in poetry?

You can have poetry as just a sort of personal notation, as a personal diary, or as a filibuster against something (usually against the readership or the audience!). But my kind of poetry, if it is poetry at all, is not that personal. It is a communication rather than a confession. It is not a confessional poetry.

D'OD: So the new circumstances in Czechoslovakia will not prompt you to be more personal in your poetry?

MH: No, not at all. [...] The scientific habit is simply not to take one's self too seriously and this is, in addition, my personal habit. I am deeply provoked by people – including poets – who take their own personalities very seriously. We should be very serious about poetry. We should be very serious about life, about survival, but not necessarily about ourselves. We are centred on our egos, anyway, instinctively, through biological necessity; but why should there be an intellectual necessity to do so? [...]

What I am defined by personally – here we are dealing with instinctive egocentrism – is that I have never had any diseases. Except as a physician, I was never in hospital and this is another thing which makes one less self-centred.

D'OD: What were your wartime experiences like?

MH: I had the good luck that at my High School we had no collaborators among the professors. We had a fantastic textbook which had to be corrected by the German influence. All the names of objectionable scientists, like Darwin, had to be blackened out with heavy lines. So we were very well-trained in ideology and anti-ideology and so have been inculcated from an early age in a very sensitive fashion.

We had a weekend house in a mountain resort in Sudetenland and my mother had to flee with a few possessions through tunnels. I was not there at the time but that was the first physical impact. The second physical impact was the bombing. Pilsen is an industrial city, so in critical periods of the war, like '44/'45 as the fronts approached, we were once or twice a week in the cellar. I am here only because I was late when I was supposed to be at Pilsen railway station on the paramedic team. The place I was supposed to be was directly hit by a bomb. Nothing was left of the room.

I have actually seen American jets fighting the Germans. I have seen American pilots abducted by Germans in April '45. German peasants in villages near Pilsen used to beat the American pilots to death with sticks. Just because of that, I saw Americans first as suffering individuals. After the war, I became a member of the American Institute and we put up a memorial; but the memorial disappeared immediately after '48. In the textbooks, the schoolkids would be told that Pilsen was liberated by the Russians. [...]

I saw people coming from the concentration camps just like cattle in open cars – as I say in the poem, 'Sunday' – their dark heads just like cutout black cardboard. This was terrible. And, of course, I did know some Jewish families who just disappeared somewhere.

D'OD: You worked on the railways during the war. What did the work consist of?

MH: First of all, I was making piles of wood. Secondly, I was working in the magazines transporting crates from the cars – very, very dirty work. Finally, I was supposed to become a clerk, so I got a telegraph training and was in a little station near Pilsen. In the event of an air-raid, I was assigned to carry the red cap of the station master and the food supply to a shelter underneath the tracks.

It was there I saw the American bombers, the bombs as little shiny bronze things falling down in a beautiful parabola and hitting from all sides the Pilsen prison. I saw the prison building rising in the air and falling apart. It was a beautiful sight, a sunny day... [...]

In poetry we have never lacked themes. If I stopped living right now there would be enough material. This you can see in any Czech writer, like Hrabal. He enlarges his life experiences by sitting in pubs and listening to people's stories, which I cannot do. I am not gifted to acquire other people's stories and to transform them. But I have enough of my own stories.

D'OD: Is simplicity something you still aspire to in poetry?

MH: Since 1963, when – having published three books of poetry in almost one year – I discovered I was talking too much, I tried to get rid of myself in a way. I began to look for other styles so as not to repeat myself. I hate to make or bake poems like rolls. All those thirty years, I have been looking for other ways of writing – sometimes more complex, more elaborate, sometimes in an entirely different form such as a little stage act or a short poem. [...]

D'OD: Did the idea of a very concrete style occur to you during your years of silence?

MH: It was a counter-style. Basically, it was a style of protest against the official poetry, which was just a poetry for May Day parades or a love poetry by well-known impotent elderly writers.

D'OD: Had you read poets like Carlos Williams at this point?

MH: Not yet. At this point, we had very few influences because after '48 very little could be imported or translated. I had a standing knowledge of French poetry, acquired in the years of freedom ('45-'47). I may have known only Jacques Prévert at that time – he was very important. It was later than this that the 'Beat' poetry came and the young Polish poets like Zbigniew Herbert and so on.

The discovery of poets like Carlos Williams was a revelation. We thought we were hidden somewhere in a little hole in central Europe under somebody's boot, under the fist of Big Brother. We had to speak with our little voices; and suddenly we discovered the little voices were being used elsewhere. This was telling us that maybe the situation was not so different elsewhere; we were not such a hidden and godforgotten place. The revelation of the San Francisco 'Beat' poets and of the Polish poets was a sort of collective discovery. The 'Beat' poet who was closest to us was Lawrence Ferlinghetti in his *Coney Island of the Mind* period and in his jazz poetry – visual, concrete, political, fighting poetry.

D'OD: Did the drugs and madness of the 'Beat' poets hold any attraction for you?

MH: In conditions of a more or less sane society, you can afford to be mad as a poet. In conditions of a mad society, you can't afford it because you would be just the establishment. You can be absurd in a non-absurd state of affairs. It is of no avail to go for absurdity in an absurd social order.

D'OD: But surrealism appealed to you, nonetheless?

MH: This was from my French connection – I was reading a lot of French poetry, especially the *poètes maudits*, up to Supervielle. This came from my mother who was a German and French professor. She loved France and as a little kid I was twice in Paris – so it was a kind of dreamland. I don't understand the present-day French poets except some like Guillevic. They are extremely introverted and I can't tell one from the other.

Surrealism was not madness in the essence, only in the vision, resulting from looking at mad things, orders, arrangements, events.

So it was a good style, a fitting vision. The inner landscape in certain periods was like a little corner of Picasso's 'Guernica' – those types of disintegration, suffering shrieks and moans.

D'OD: What was the effect on your poetry of a classical training?

MH: Czech literary classes were very scholarly: years, titles and so on. But in Greek and Latin, we had to read epics all year – *Iliad* and *Odyssey* and the *Bucolics*. We would learn it by heart so the heroes like Menelaus or Agamemnon or Achilles became just like our inner property. I was always feeling sorry for Patroclus.

D'OD: Did your determination to work towards single books rather than single poems derive from your study of those classical texts?

MH: No, it's just a reaction against the subjective way of making poetic collections as a sort of physiological function of the lunar cycles of a poet – you simply shed some poems and later you collect them in a bunch and say, 'This was the state of my soul for the last year.' More and more I hate it.

D'OD: Generally speaking, has poetry played a large part in modern Czechoslovakian life?

MH: From '56 to '68, with the Khrushchev liberalisation and so on, the literary life really started. There was a general feeling of progress. In this period, poetry was one of the leading arts. Very much of what happened in lyrical theatre forms, in TV, and in other literary forms had a strong poetic basis. After '68, when so many things were dilapidated and banned, I thought it would be interesting to see how the other arts will do without poetry. There were full-grown walls between arts and between persons. In the 70s and 80s, it never attained the status it had in the 60s. [...]

D'OD: Were you surprised at the suddenness with which Communism crumbled in late '89?

MH: The spirit of the 60s was progress. The 70s for everybody brought a hopeless situation. People like Havel just had the guts and the nerve and the audacity and the human quality of self-sacrifice.

In the mid-70s, when I was a non-person, I was told by the great Czech actor, Jan Werich, 'You must write. Intellectuality, irony and satire are what we need for survival. We don't need lyrical, emotional or even political poems; we need something more incisive.' Cracks were visible already since '86 or '87, but that the system was already powder I wouldn't have thought. [...]

Extract from April 1990 interview first published in *Krino* (Autumn 1990).

In the microscope

Here too are dreaming landscapes,
lunar, derelict.
Here too are the masses,
tillers of the soil.
And cells, fighters
who lay down their lives
for a song.
Here too are cemeteries,
fame and snow.
And I hear murmuring,
the revolt of immense estates.

[1958] IM

The corporal who killed Archimedes

With one bold stroke
he killed the circle, tangent
and point of intersection
in infinity.

On penalty
of quartering
he banned numbers
from three up.

Now in Syracuse
he heads a school of philosophers,
squats on his halberd
for another thousand years
and writes:

one two
one two
one two
one two

[1960] IM/JM

Five minutes after the air raid

In Pilsen,
twenty-six Station Road,
she climbed to the third floor
up stairs which were all that was left
of the whole house,
she opened her door
full on to the sky,
stood gaping over the edge.

For this was the place
the world ended.

Then
she locked up carefully
lest someone steal
Sirius
or Aldebaran
from her kitchen,
went back downstairs
and settled herself
to wait
for the house to rise again
and for her husband to rise from the ashes
and for her children's hands and feet to be stuck back in place.

In the morning they found her
still as stone,
sparrows pecking her hands.

[1960] GT

The fly

She sat on a willow-trunk
watching
part of the battle of Crécy,
the shouts,
the gasps,
the groans,
the tramping and the tumbling.

During the fourteenth charge
'of the French cavalry
she mated
with a brown-eyed male fly
from Vadincourt.

She rubbed her legs together
as she sat on a disembowelled horse
meditating
on the immortality of flies.

With relief she alighted
on the blue tongue
of the Duke of Clervaux.

When silence settled
and only the whisper of decay
softly circled the bodies

and only
a few arms and legs
still twitched jerkily under the trees,

she began to lay her eggs
on the single eye
of Johann Uhr,
the Royal Armourer.

And thus it was
that she was eaten by a swift
fleeing
from the fires of Estrées.

[1961] GT

Polonius

Behind every arras
he does his duty
unswervingly.
Walls are his ears,
keyholes his eyes.

43

He slinks up the stairs,
oozes from the ceiling,
floats through the door
ready to give evidence,
prove what is proven,
stab with a needle
or pin on an order.

His poems always rhyme,
his brush is dipped in honey,
his music flutes
from marzipan and cane.

You buy him
by weight, boneless,
a pound of wax flesh,
a pound of mousy philosophy,
a pound of jellied
flunkey.

And when he's sold out
and the leftovers wrapped
in a tasselled obituary,
a paranoid funeral notice,

and when the spore-creating mould
of memory
covers him over,
when he falls
arse-first to the stars,

the whole continent will be lighter,
earth's axis straighten up
and in night's thunderous arena
a bird will chirp in gratitude.

[1961] IM

A helping hand

We gave a helping hand to grass –
    and it turned into corn.
We gave a helping hand to fire –
    and it turned into a rocket.

44

Hesitatingly,
cautiously,
we give a helping hand
to people,
to some people...

[1961] GT

The door

Go and open the door.
  Maybe outside there's
  a tree, or a wood,
  a garden,
  or a magic city.

Go and open the door.
  Maybe a dog's rummaging.
  Maybe you'll see a face,
or an eye,
or the picture
              of a picture.

Go and open the door.
  If there's a fog
  it will clear.

Go and open the door.
  Even if there's only
  the darkness ticking,
  even if there's only
  the hollow wind,
  even if
          nothing
                  is there,
go and open the door.

At least
there'll be
a draught.

[1961] IM

What the heart is like

Officially the heart
is oblong, muscular,
and filled with longing.

But anyone who has painted the heart knows
that it is also

spiked like a star
and sometimes bedraggled
like a stray dog at night
and sometimes powerful
like an archangel's drum.

And sometimes cube-shaped
like a draughtsman's dream
and sometimes gaily round
like a ball in a net.

And sometimes like a thin line
and sometimes like an explosion.

And in it is
only a river,
a weir
and at most one little fish
by no means golden.

More like a grey
jealous
loach.

It certainly isn't noticeable
at first sight.

Anyone who has painted the heart knows
that first he had to
discard his spectacles,
his mirror,
throw away his fine-point pencil
and carbon paper

and for a long while
walk
outside.

[1963] EO

The end of the world

The bird had come to the very end of its song
and the tree was dissolving under its claws.

And in the sky the clouds were twisting
and darkness flowed through all the cracks
into the sinking vessel of the landscape.

Only in the telegraph wires
a message still
crackled:

C·—·—·o———m——e· h···o———m——e·
y—·——o———u··— h···a·—v····—e·
a·— s···o———n—.

[1963] EO

A boy's head

In it there is a space-ship
and a project
for doing away with piano lessons.

And there is
Noah's ark,
which shall be first.

And there is
an entirely new bird,
an entirely new hare,
an entirely new bumble-bee.

There is a river
that flows upwards.

There is a multiplication table.

There is anti-matter.

And it just cannot be trimmed.

I believe
that only what cannot be trimmed
is a head.

There is much promise
in the circumstance
that so many people have heads.

[1963] IM

The Prague of Jan Palach

And here stomp Picasso's bulls.
And here march Dalí's elephants on spidery legs.
And here beat Schönberg's drums.
And here rides Señor de la Mancha.
And here the Karamazovs are carrying Hamlet.
And here is the nucleus of the atom.
And here is the cosmodrome of the Moon.
And here stands a statue without the torch.
And here runs a torch without the statue.
And it's all so simple. Where
Man ends, the flame begins –
And in the ensuing silence can be heard the crumbling
of ash worms. For
those milliards of people, taken by and large,
are keeping their traps shut.

[UK 1969] GT

Brief reflection on accuracy

Fish
   always accurately know where to move and when,
   and likewise
   birds have an accurate built-in time sense
   and orientation.

Humanity, however,
   lacking such instincts resorts to scientific
   research. Its nature is illustrated by the following
   occurrence.

A certain soldier
   had to fire a cannon at six o'clock sharp every evening.
   Being a soldier he did so. When his accuracy was
   investigated he explained:

I go by
   the absolutely accurate chronometer in the window
   of the clockmaker down in the city. Every day at seventeen
   forty-five I set my watch by it and
   climb the hill where my cannon stands ready.
   At seventeen fifty-nine precisely I step up to the cannon
   and at eighteen hours sharp I fire.

And it was clear
   that this method of firing was absolutely accurate.
   All that was left was to check that chronometer. So
   the clockmaker down in the city was questioned about
   his instrument's accuracy.

Oh, said the clockmaker,
   this is one of the most accurate instruments ever. Just imagine,
   for many years now a cannon has been fired at six o'clock sharp.
   And every day I look at this chronometer
   and always it shows exactly six.

So much for accuracy.
   And fish move in the water, and from the skies
   comes a rushing of wings while

Chronometers tick and cannon boom.

[1982] EO

49

Conversation with a poet

Are you a poet?
    Yes, I am.
How do you know?
    I've written poems.
If you've written poems it means you *were* a poet. But now?
    I'll write a poem again one day.
In that case maybe you'll be a poet again one day. But how will you
know it is a poem?
    It will be a poem just like the last one.
Then of course it won't be a poem. A poem is only once and can
never be the same a second time.
    I believe it will be just as good.
How can you be sure? Even the quality of a poem is for once only
and depends not on you but on circumstances.
    I believe that circumstances will be the same too.
If you believe that then you won't be a poet and never were a poet.
What then makes you think you are a poet?
    Well – I don't rightly know. And who are you?

[1982] EO

A lecture on arthropods

The mite Adactylidium
hatches in his mother's body,
eats up his mother's body from inside
while mating
with all his seven
little sisters.

So that when he's born
it's just as if he had died:
he's been through it all

and is freelancing now
in the target's bull's-eye,
at the focus of non-obligatory existence:

50

an absolute poet,
non-segmented,
non-antenniferous,
eight-legged.

[1986] EO

Half a hedgehog

The rear half had been run over,
leaving the head and thorax
and the front legs of the hedgehog shape.

A scream from a cramped-open
jaw. The scream of the mute is
more horrible than the silence after a flood,
when even black swans float
belly upwards.

And even if some hedgehog doctor were
to be found in a hollow trunk or under the leaves
in a beechwood there'd be no hope
for that mere half on Road E12.

In the name of logic,
in the name of the theory of pain,
in the name of the hedgehog god the father, the son
and the holy ghost amen,
in the name of games and unripe raspberries,
in the name of tumbling streams of love
ever different and ever bloody,
in the name of the roots which overgrow
the heads of aborted foetuses,
in the name of satanic beauty,
in the name of skin bearing human likeness,
in the name of all halves
and double helices, or purines
and pyrimidines

we tried to run over
the hedgehog's head with the front wheel.

And it was like guiding a lunar module
from a planetary distance,
from a control centre seized
by cataleptic sleep.

And the mission failed. I got out
and found a heavy piece of brick.
Half the hedgehog continued screaming. And now
the scream turned into speech,

prepared by
the vaults of our tombs:
Then death will come and it will have your eyes.

[1986] EO

The dead

After his third operation, his heart
riddled like an old fairground target,
he woke up on his bed
and said: Now I'll be fine,
fit as a fiddle. And have you ever seen
horses coupling?

He died that night.

And another dragged on through eight insipid years
like a river weed in an acid stream,
as if pushing up his pallid
skewered face over the cemetery wall.

Until that face eventually vanished.

Both here and there the angel of death
quite simply stamped his hobnailed boot
on their medulla oblongata.

I know they died the same way.
But I don't believe they are
dead the same way.

[1986] EO

Distant howling

In Alsace,
on 6th July 1885,
a rabid dog knocked down
the nine-year-old Joseph Meister
and bit him fourteen times.

Meister was the first patient
saved by Pasteur
with his vaccine, in thirteen
progressive doses
of the attenuated virus.

Pasteur died of ictus
ten years later.
The janitor Meister
fifty-five years later
committed suicide
when the Germans occupied
his Pasteur Institute
with all those poor dogs.

Only the virus
remained above it all.

[1986] EO

At last

At last we were masters of our heads,
masters of the city,
masters of our shadows
and our equinox.

Someone fired a shot to celebrate,
but only the kind with a cork
tied to a string.

And then we opened the cages
and ferrets ran out.
Out of the skull ran brown and white
spotted rats.
Out of the heart flew
blood-soaked cuckoos.

Out of the lungs
a condor rose, croaking with rage
because of the way his plumes had been squashed
in the bronchi.

Even a panther showed up,
on the loose from an obsolete circus,
starved, ready to eat
even the Emperor Claudius.

You could hear squeaks in the streets –
the groans and shouts
of expiring fiends.

And at last we were masters
of our new moon.

But we couldn't step out
of our doorways;
someone might cast
a spell on us.

We might even
be hostage
to ourselves.

[1998] MH/DY

Translators: [IM] Ian Milner. [IM/IM] Ian & Jarmila Milner. [EO] Ewald
Osers. [GT] George Theiner. [MH/DY] Miroslav Holub & David Young.

Dates: Year of first publication of original Czech poem in book form. Poems
first collected in 1982 were written in 1971-82; poems first collected in 1986
were written in 1983-86. 'The Prague of Jan Palach' was first published in 1969
in English but not published in Czech until after 1989.

MARIN SORESCU

Marin Sorescu (1936-96) was a cheerfully melancholic comic genius, and one of the most original voices in Romanian literature. His mischievous poetry and satirical plays earned him great popularity during the Communist era. While his witty, ironic parables were not directly critical of the régime, Romanians used to a culture of double-speak could read other meanings in his playful mockery of the human condition. But later – like a hapless character from one of his absurdist dramas – the peasant-born people's poet was made Minister of Culture, in Ion Iliescu's post-Ceauşescu government.

Like Holub, Sorescu used plain, deceptively straightforward language, believing that poetry should be 'concise, almost algebraic'. Seamus Heaney wrote that behind Sorescu's 'throwaway charm and poker-faced subversiveness...there is a persistent solidarity with the unregarded life of the ordinary citizen, a willingness to remain at eye-level and on a speaking terms with common experience'.

A prolific writer and a prominent dramatist, Sorescu published over 20 books of poetry in Romania, with several English translations of his poetry and plays appearing in Britain and America. Michael

Hamburger's translation of his *Selected Poems* (1983), drawing on six collections published between 1965 and 1973, introduced him to English readers. *The Biggest Egg in the World* followed in 1987, a selection of mostly later work edited by Edna Longley with translators including Ted Hughes, Seamus Heaney and Paul Muldoon.

Virgil Nemoianu has described how Sorescu's black humour and keen feeling for the absurd enabled him to survive as a writer: 'His reactions to an increasingly absurd political régime were always cleverly balanced: he never engaged in the servile praise of leader and party usually required of Romanian poets, but nor did he venture into dissidence. He was content to let irony do its job... His texts are masterpieces of allusion and adroit manoeuvring...' All this time, however, he was also writing the 'secret poems' he dared not publish then because – as Dan Zamfirescu commented – 'the gesture would have been the equivalent of suicide'. *Censored Poems* (2001), translated by John Hartley Williams and Hilde Ottschofski, is a selection from two books published in Bucharest after 1989, including borderline poems censored by the authorities as well as the risker secret poems censored by the author.

The Bridge (2004), translated by Adam J. Sorkin and Lidia Vianu, published in Romania in 1997, was Sorescu's farewell to life, a book of painfully quizzical poems composed from his sickbed over five weeks as he waited for death to take him. He died from liver cancer on 8 December 1996, in the same year that he was nominated for the Nobel Prize for Literature.

Marin Sorescu was born in the village of Bulzeşti, Dolj, in the south of Romania, the fifth child of a family of peasants; his father – an avid reader – died when he was three. He published his first poems in 1959, in magazines. After studying Russian and then Romanian at the University of Iaşi, he became editor in 1963 of the literary journal *Luceafărul*, and from 1966 to 1972 was editor-in-chief of the Animafilm Cinematographic Studios.

He was able to take up overseas residencies from time to time, including at the University of Iowa (1970-71) and in West Berlin (1973-74 and 1990), and received many national and international literary awards. From 1978 he edited the literary review *Ramuri*, and in 1990 founded a new journal, *Literatorul*; he was also director of the Romanian Writer Publishing House. He usually managed to avoid direct conflict with the authorities, although in the early 1980s he was sentenced to three months of house arrest, and ran into difficulties over his work; 150 pages were cut from a large novel published in 1977. At times when he could not publish or, later in the difficult 1980s, felt very restricted, Sorescu, who had always drawn and doodled, often illustrating his books, began oil-painting with seriousness; his first one-man show was in Braşov in 1989.

Introducing his work to a Berlin audience in 1990, Sorescu commented ruefully on the censors' role in shaping his output: 'Since my very first book, I have been a client of the censor's. Irony is suspicious, and so is jokes... Everything I wrote was put under the microscope. Many poems were continually returned with the explanation "it isn't the right moment" or "these verses could be interpreted". I was able to put some of them into later books. Some I didn't dare to print – on the contrary I hid them so well that even today I'm unable to find them...The permanent catastrophe of being delivered up to censorship has its good side. You're sure to find a pair of faithful and attentive readers.'

Four Perspectives on Sorescu

1. MICHAEL HAMBURGER

Like many Eastern European poets who began to write after the war, Sorescu felt it necessary to make a clean break with the Romantic-Symbolist assumptions that had dominated Western poetry up to that time, when French culture exercised a powerful influence in Romania. The officially prescribed alternative, "socialist realism", proved of little use to lyric poets...Those with more independence of mind tended towards a "minimal poetry", often elliptic, laconic, depersonalised, or masked under an assumed impersonality.

Sorescu's alternative was a freedom of invention that could strike superficial readers as "surrealist". Yet Sorescu's procedures are as far removed as possible from surrealism, despite the dream-like situations set up in many of his poems. Surrealism demanded a liberation of the subconscious and aspired to automatic writing. Sorescu's verse parables approach human realities by way of fantasy and irony; not, however, to liberate the subconscious, his own or anyone else's, but rather to arrive at truths that have to do with human existence on a conscious level. It is the interplay of fantasy and irony that sets his work as far apart from surrealism as from a mimetic photographic realism.

From introduction to *Selected Poems* (Bloodaxe Books, 1983).

2. EDNA LONGLEY

Perhaps Sorescu's poems adapt so readily to translation by many hands because they are themselves a form of translation, even of

Esperanto. He translates everyday phenomena, common experiences, into their emblematic contours. 'It is time to learn from the bats...' Always, as in 'Map', we follow the pointer. While Sorescu's parables are mysteries and riddles, they are also clarifications and answers. They have the universal accessibility with which fables override linguistic boundaries. The imagery, deceptively casual in its cosmic reach, maps a universe in which 'Destiny' gives human beings little room to manoeuvre – or to do anything except manoeuvre.

The structure of the poems, too, both explores and imitates ironic collisions between free will and fate. Whether or not this reflects an unadmitted social or political context, Sorescu is raising large moral and metaphysical questions...Throughout *The Biggest Egg in the World* the resilient and resourceful artistic personality of Marin Sorescu powerfully unites all the guises it assumes.

From foreword to *The Biggest Egg in the World* (Bloodaxe Books, 1987).

3. JOHN HARTLEY WILLIAMS

For most of his adult life, Marin Sorescu practised the art of poetry under a régime that tolerated his preoccupations, whilst condemning them as bourgeois frivolity. On condition writers and artists could accept the Machiavellian reasons for their own survival, and did not protest too much, they were useful token ambassadors for governments which did not subscribe to "humanistic" values. Sorescu's work was even promoted by the régime. He was a clown (they thought), and what's more he was popular. Sorescu must have understood the kind of pact with the devil he was making, but what choice did he have? He could have shut up completely (a project he certainly entertained), or he could have become openly defiant, had his books banned, and suffered long terms in prison. He chose to continue writing and to walk the difficult line between outright revolt and self-imposed censorship. [...]

What made Sorescu jump out of his skin, as the poems in this collection attest, was patriotic fury. He had to stand by and watch as his country was slowly destroyed. Ceauşescu's hatred of the peasantry, the stock from which Sorescu himself sprang, caused villages to be bulldozed and peasant farmers uprooted. Those by-words of historical materialism – modernisation, industrialisation – were the meaningless catchwords of a political programme that was empty and sterile. There was nothing to put in the place of the bulldozed villages except the vacuum of the régime itself, corrupt, self-seeking and dismally stupid. [...]

And although Sorescu can sometimes employ vicious mockery –
for example at those who have connived at the suspension of the
rule of law and are then horrified and shocked to find the hangman's
noose round their own necks (see the poems 'Pleasant executions'
and 'The report'), taken as a whole, these poems reveal not so much
the sarcastic side of Sorescu as the fragile yet devout person who
yearns for death and resurrection, and believes in natural retribution
and hell. He has a powerful sense of identification with the natural
world, with the forests, animals and birds who represent the good
and the incorruptible on this tainted planet. They exert a Buddhist
level of acceptance and calm on him. The poems set the "honesty"
of the natural world against the viciousness of the human one [...]

Artists in "socialist" Eastern Europe could enjoy the particular
benevolence of the state if they delivered the "message". Poetry
was supposed to mobilise, praise and incite, in a word, 'speak to
the readers' hearts' although, as Sorescu commented, 'where exactly
the aestheticians of the hour localised the readers' hearts was
difficult to say – as this kind of poetry never connected with the
normal place, under the breast'. Like all true poets, Sorescu had a
twofold mission. He wanted to preserve language, and transform
life. His working tool was the imagination. He had no programme,
no agit-prop message. His ideology was a belief in the transforming
power of words, imaginatively used, and to readers conditioned to
literalism he could only mutter exasperatedly:

> This craving for transparency,
> it shreds my nerves...

Opposed always to the blatant purposes of social engineering
which afflict "official" poetry wherever such poetry appears, Sorescu's
poems hold up to our gaze a world in which human affairs seem
perpetually doomed to descend to the level of a tragic buffoonery.
The poet who writes them is a volatile character, despairing one
minute, celebrating the next – his mood-swings are alarming. He
can be devastatingly direct, and then *chop* – logically complicated
and obscure. Sorescu himself remarked: 'When I no longer know
who I am, I re-read my poems to find out.'

From introduction to *Censored Poems* (Bloodaxe Books, 2001).

4. ADAM J. SORKIN

During the last two months of his life, he wrote prolifically. These
poems, with their dedication, *To all who suffer*, are a testament not
just to human mortality and pain but to resistance and triumph, a

creative transformation of the struggle to accept fate and in the same breath defy its imminent finality. Sorescu composed poetry until the day before he died. Too weak to write, or, as the end came near, too downhearted – on his final day, he told his wife Virginia, 'I feel something that I never had before,' which she understood as a sign from him – he increasingly required her help to put on paper many of these valedictory works.

The Bridge is Sorescu's deathbed book, his consummation, and he of course knew this. Except for two poems inserted into the rest from when he was in a Paris hospital in October 1996, the volume progresses chronologically from the beginning of November onward. A mere five weeks. Most of the poems are dated, and the inexorable momentum of poem after poem toward Sorescu's death seems to make of the book something like a medieval tableau, a dance of death arranged as a procession of still living poems. [...]

Throughout *The Bridge*, expressions of doubt, reluctant faith, protest, pain and despair mingle with what – as a translator and long-time reader of Sorescu's works – I see as gestures toward his characteristic ironic pose, flights into the fabulous and fanciful that, in context, are neither comically detached nor humorous in spirit. The blackness of the black humour is perhaps too urgent, too real. Within the world of the book, even given the parabolic, absurdist artifice of a substantial number of the poems, the poet's voice projects a verbal space free of pretence. Sorescu's typically wry, deadpan stance here turns inward and transparent. Many of the poems forego the playfulness of verbal irony (though the writer's situation is saturated with dramatic irony, every word defying the future); roughly three dozen of the 75 poems are spare and direct, as if in his final weeks simplicity became as expressive a tonality as the calculated ambiguity of poetic disguise and indirection. [...]

The book repeatedly gives rise to an emotional and artistic tension between, on the one hand, the pathetic and the sombre and, on the other, though not really in antithesis, the comic, the whimsical and the tongue-in-cheek. Marin Sorescu the genial, worldly-wise man of the theatre, who in his poetry is always close by the lyrical persona, waiting in the wings for his cue, performs a beguiling, anti-heroic, anti-sentimental role before bringing the curtain down – and completely steals the show. His canny, seemingly guileless voice is paradoxically the mask of a hard-earned authenticity. Translating *The Bridge* ultimately became a humbling experience, an act of especial homage and respect.

From foreword to *The Bridge* (Bloodaxe Books, 2004).

'With a green scarf'

With a green scarf I blindfolded
the eyes of the trees
and asked them to catch me.

At once the trees caught me,
their leaves shaking with laughter.

I blindfolded the birds
with a scarf of clouds
and asked them to catch me.

The birds caught me
with a song.

Then with a smile I blindfolded
my sorrow
and the day after it caught me
with a love.

I blindfolded the sun
with my nights
and asked the sun to catch me.

I know where you are, the sun said,
just behind that time.
Don't bother to hide any longer.

Don't bother to hide any longer,
said all of them,
as well as all the feelings
I tried to blindfold.

[1965] MH

Sorescu translators: [DC] David Constantine. [DJE] D.J. Enright.
[MH] Michael Hamburger. [SH] Seamus Heaney. [IRG] Ioana Russell-Gebbett.
[PM] Paul Muldoon. [AJS/LV] Adam J. Sorkin & Lidia Vianu.
[JHW/HO] John Hartley Williams & Hilde Ottschofski.

Dates: Year of first publication of original poem in book form in Romania.
Dates after poems from *The Bridge* (1997) show when they were written.

Superstition

My cat washes
with her left paw,
there will be another war.

For I have observed
that whenever she washes
with her left paw
international tension grows
considerably.

How can she possibly keep her eye
on all the five continents?
Could it be
that in her pupils
that Pythia now resides
who has the power
to predict
the whole of history
without a full-stop or comma?

It's enough to make me howl
when I think that I
and the Heaven with its souls I have
shouldered
in the last resort
depend
on the whims of a cat.

Go and catch mice,
don't unleash
more world wars,
damned
lazybones!

[1966] MH

Pond

The pond was a deep pond once,
The baits hung down

Like fruit, like shining fruit, lanterns,
Attainable planets and we
Went busily choosing a heart's delight
For the size of our mouths and rose flapping
Like Angels. Now
Here we are in a crowd
In a muddy six inches gasping
For worms and the shadows
Of peering fisherman
Have quite put out the light.

[1968] DC/IRG

Adam

Although he was in Paradise,
Adam walked the paths preoccupied and sad,
Not knowing what he was missing.

Then God fashioned Eve
From one of Adam's ribs.
And the first man liked this miracle so much
That right away
He touched the adjacent rib,
Sensing a delicate tingling in his fingers
From firm breasts and sweet hips
Like the contours of music.
A new Eve had risen in front of him.
She had taken her little mirror out
And was painting her mouth.
'That's life!' sighed Adam,
And created another one.

And thus, whenever the official Eve
Turned her back,
Or went to the market for gold and incense and myrrh,
Adam brought an extra odalisque to life
From his intercostal harem.

God had observed
This disorderly creativity of Adam's.
He summoned him, denounced him divinely,

And expelled him from Paradise
For surrealism.

[1968] DJE/IRG

Friends

Come on, let's kill ourselves, I say to my friends.
Today we communicated so well,
we were all so sad,
never again shall we rise to
that point of perfection together;
to hesitate now would be a sin.

In the bath, I believe, it's most tragic,
so let's do it the way the enlightened Romans did it,
opening their veins
while discoursing on the nature of love.
Friends, the water's been heated,
let's begin, I will count: one, two, three...

Not without astonishment I noted in Hell
that I was on my own.
For some it's harder, I told myself,
some have all sorts of ties;
it can't be that they were making a fool of me: a man's word counts
        for something,
but the passage of time...

True enough, Hell wasn't a bed of roses for me,
especially at first, with nobody about
I could really talk to,
but gradually I found company, made friends.

A circle quite extraordinarily close-knit.
We discussed a number of theories,
felt in excellent spirits
and even got as far as suicide.

...And again I found myself alone, in Purgatory.
Looking around, for a kindred soul or two,

and yet, although the occupants of Purgatory,
in their inter-territorial uncertainty,
are very prone to suspicion –
a girl is fond of me, she loves me, she's good-looking,
we have moments of great ecstasy. It's incredible, marvellous!

I'm about to propose...
Knowing better now, I leave it to her,
before taking the plunge.
The girl does what she does, and is alive again –
and I'm alone in Heaven.
Never has anyone got this far,
I am the first, the world exists as a project;
a very vague affair
in the mind of God,
with whom meanwhile I have made friends.

On all levels, it seems, there is sadness.
God is in despair,
I gaze into his empty eyes and lose myself.
He whirls into the chasms of my deaths.
We understand each other splendidly,
my God, I believe it couldn't be better.
It's your turn. Or what do you say
to leaving it all in the dark?

[1970] MH

The Thieves

One of my poems kept me awake at night,
so I sent it into the country
to a grandfather.

After that I wrote another
and sent it to my mother
to store in her attic.

I still wrote several more
and with misgivings entrusted them to relations
who promised to keep them with care.

And so forth; for every new poem
there was someone to take it in.
Since each of my friends
in his turn has
a friend he keeps quiet about.

And now even I don't remember
where this and that line might be,
and if I were to fall among thieves
and they tortured me too, the most I could tell them
is that those dubious things
are somewhere in the country
and safe.

[1972] MH

Heritage

From antiquity, from
The Middle Ages, from
All of history, anywhere,
Whole trainloads of errors
Addressed to us
Are still rolling in.

Tactical and strategical errors,
Political errors,
Gaffes of every sort,
Imbecilities, clangers,
Insignificant slips
Or drastic misjudgements.
On every track they're coming in,
By day and by night, round the clock,
So that pointsmen are suffering nervous breakdowns,

While we, the laughing heirs,
Only keep on unloading
And signing receipts for the stuff.

[1975] MH

Precautions

I pulled on a suit of mail
made of pebbles
worn smooth by water.

I balanced a pair of glasses
on my neck
so as to keep an eye
on whatever
was coming behind me.

I gloved and greaved
my hands, my legs, my thoughts
leaving no part of my person
exposed to touch
or other poisons.

Then I fashioned a breastplate
from the shell
of an eight-hundred-year-old
turtle.

And when everything was just so
I tenderly replied:
– I love you too.

[1975] PM/IRG

The tear

I weep and weep a tear
Which will not fall
No matter how much I weep.

Its pang in me
Is like the birth of an icicle.

Colder and colder, the earth

Curves on my eyelid,
The northern ice-cap keeps rising.

O, my arctic eyelid.

[1982] SH/IRG

The sentence

Each new passenger, on the tramcar,
is a carbon-copy of the one who occupied
the seat before him.

Either we're moving too fast
or the world's too small.

Everyone's neck is chafed
by the newspaper whoever's behind him's reading.
If I turned round right now
I'd be cutting
my own throat.

[1982] PM/IRG

Competition

One, two, three...
Here begins the hibernation contest.
All of you shut yourselves up in your holes,
And we shall see who hibernates the longest.

You know the rules of the competition:
You are not allowed to move,
You are not allowed to dream,
You are not allowed to think.
Anyone caught thinking
Is out of the game and no longer of interest.

You may only suck your paw
Like a pipe,

68

Which stimulates you to a profound understanding of
The phenomenon.

I am lucky to find myself next to a bear,
And when I get fed up with my own paw
I shall pass it on to him,
Taking his in exchange,
Which – as it happens – falls within the limits of
Permitted paws.

And though the Pharaoh Cheops
Has a start of several millennia,
I hope to overtake even him
With a formidable sprint,
Our celebrated sprint
In the sphere of hibernation.

[1982] DJE/IRG

SIX PRE-1989 POEMS FROM *CENSORED POEMS* [JHW/HO]:

Impressions

The butcher's shop is closed. A sign
proclaims: *Gone to the Meeting.*
'I've no meat,' the butcher tells the meeting.
Someone writes this down, to shop him.

Our informer, eager to improve the tale,
minces into the meatlessness several
cloven hooves, forked tails, and horns.
A modest dish, he thinks, and smirks.

There's nothing at the market but the market.
A pack of rats and a fishwife, who whacks
a broom at them and drives them off with shrieks –

or tries to trap them with a fishy skeleton,
raised from the Dead Sea, they say, by a thread.
Welcome to the witches' brew of Bucharest.

House under surveillance

They've come to take my manuscripts away
with a crane as tall as a tree.
I open the doors of the pages, set free
my poems. They soar into the sky.

Lead pellets fired through telescopes
wound the rhythms of those beating wings.
My stanzas fall. With twisted grins
the hunters fire again. The words are killed.

Greasy palm upon his gun butt,
the guard is watching you, my heart.
You could be silenced with a single shot

and this house they've set on fire
is the dream to which you cling.
Become a poem only if you must.

Here

I'm here, I'm nowhere.
The house itself is persecuted
into building walls of silence
which it must stand behind, locked in.

Locked inside myself, I haven't given up.
Give me gibberish, babble, double talk –
let equivocation be sweet on my tongue!
Then a raven croaks: *Nevermore!*

The gleam vanishes off the world.
This blind, ravening century has put
its mark upon the very bread we eat.

Anything I say will be interpreted
by thugs. The cop on guard outside
is trying to get my spaniel to confess.

The martyrs

Just the usual lion-fodder, no one
whose name will ever make the calendar,
anonymously rattling into death.

Fed to bestial mud, your bodies are
frail as flowers. The life that you enjoy
will have to be the next one.

To carry off a crucifixion, talent
is required. It takes skill, as well, to plunge a trident
deep in someone's throat. The goggling
crowd awaits the miracle to follow,

which won't, of course, take place.
There's just an ugly pool of blood
where the ripped-to-pieces die. That's it.
Matinees on Tuesdays. Bring a friend.

The Impaler speaks

Transpierced, in agony, you're like
manure on a fork. When a seed
is planted in the ground,
it needs a hole, driven in.

No atrocity, no apocalyptic
anguish could be like this.
I take the comet's whip, and
brand your shoulder with a lily.

My character was steeped in sloth.
Elected as your ruler, I starved myself
of sleep and rest in penance,
to show the world this princely face.

You, you're soused in such a stupefying
idleness, I have no means to heal it.
But deep in hell a lake of pitch awaits
to drown you in its fire a millionfold.

The Arrow

Wounded, he'd have
been lost in the forest,
had he not followed the arrow.

More than half
of it
protruded from his chest
and showed him the way.

The arrow
had struck him in the back
and pierced his body.
Its bloodied tip
was a signpost.

What a blessing
to have it point
a path
between the trees!

Now he knew
he'd never again
go wrong

and he
wasn't far
from the mark.

FOUR POEMS FROM *THE BRIDGE* [AJS/LV]:

A Ladder to the Sky

A spider's thread
Hangs from the ceiling,
Directly over my bed.

Every day I keep track of
How much closer it descends.
'Look,' I say to myself,
'I'm being sent a ladder to the sky,
Lowered from above.'

I've grown dreadfully thin,
A mere ghost of what I used to be,
Yet I think my body
Is too heavy still
For this delicate ladder.

'Soul, you go ahead.
Shhh! Shhh!'

[5 November 1996]

Pure Pain

I don't feel ill in order to feel better,
I feel ill in order to feel worse.
Like the sea with its green, treacherous waves,
You cannot sound the bottom of pain.

I dive into pure pain,
Essence of scream and despair,
And I return to the surface blue and pale,
Like a diver who lost
His oxygen tank.

To the emperor of fishes, I beg,
Kindly send me your most trustworthy shark
To cut short my passing.

[6 November 1996]

Prayer of the Heart

Lord,
Help me as long as
I still live.

Set my heart in order,
Put me at peace with the world
And the miracle of life.

Remove from my mind
The fixed idea
Which has imprisoned me.

Make of my subconscious
A torrent of hope.

[*5 December 1996*]

'I am reminded of all our dogs'

I am reminded of
All our dogs
When it came time to die
Of old age.
They would lie hidden under the shed,
Under the corn crib.
You'd take them food, water.
Slowly, they would open their eyelids,
They would look, they would raise their eyes
Toward you,
Then they would close them once again.
And they couldn't even wag
Their tail once,
To thank you.

Terrible is the passage
Into the fold
Both for man and for animal.

[*7 December 1996*]

TOMAS TRANSTRÖMER

Sweden's **Tomas Tranströmer** has been called a 'buzzard poet' (by Lasse Söderberg) because his haunting, visionary poetry shows the world from a height, in a mystic dimension, but brings every detail of the natural world into sharp focus. His poems are often explorations of the borderland between sleep and waking, between the conscious and unconscious states.

He is Scandinavia's best-known and most influential contemporary poet. His books sell thousands of copies in Sweden, and his work has been translated into 50 languages, with substantial or complete editions of his work published in 19 languages.

Tranströmer was born in 1931 in Stockholm, where he grew up, but spent many long summers on the island of Runmarö in the nearby archipelago, evoking that landscape in his early work, which draws on the aesthetic tradition of Swedish nature poetry. His later poetry is more personal, open and relaxed, often reflecting his broad interests: travel, music, painting, archaeology and natural sciences.

Many of his poems use compressed description and concentrate on a single distinct image as a catalyst for psychological insight and metaphysical interpretation. This acts as a meeting-point or threshold between conflicting elements or forces: sea and land, man and nature, freedom and control. His translator Robin Fulton has

75

noted how such images 'leap out from the page, so that the first-time reader or listener has the feeling of being given something very tangible, at once', which has made Tranströmer's poetry amenable to translation into other languages. But while acknowledging Tranströmer's view that 'a poem can exist beneath or prior to a particular language and can therefore emerge in any number of tongues', Fulton maintains that 'the best versions of his poems are those he made himself in his own language'. Yet such is the power of Tranströmer's 'deep image' poetry that several American poets have been influenced by his work, through translations by Robert Bly in particular.

Tranströmer started writing poetry while at the oppressive Södra Latin Grammar School (its atmosphere caught by Ingmar Bergman in Alf Sjöberg's *Frenzy*, which was filmed there, the young Tomas amongst the pupils). But he was devouring books on all subjects, especially geography, with daily visits to the local library, where he worked his way through most of the non-fiction shelves. However, this bookish adolescence was shadowed by the war, by his parents' divorce and the absence of his father, and at 15 he experienced a winter of psychological crisis (described in 'Exorcism'). He published his first collection, *17 Poems*, in 1954, at the age of 23.

After studying psychology at the University of Stockholm, he worked at its Psychotechnological Institute, and in 1960 became a psychologist at Roxtuna, a young offenders institution. From the mid-1960s he divided his time between his writing and his work as a psychologist, and in 1965 moved with his family to Västerås, where he spent the rest of his working life.

Like the scientist-poet Miroslav Holub, Tranströmer sees no division between his own two fields, poetry and psychology. In an interview in 1973 he responded to Gunnar Harding's question about how his writing related to his work as a psychologist:

> I believe there is a very close connection, though it can't be seen. Everything one writes is an expression of a gathered experience. And the problems one meets in the world at large are present to a very great extent in what I write, though it doesn't always show directly. But it's close to hand, all the time.

In 1990, a year after the publication of his tenth book of poems, Tranströmer suffered a stroke, which deprived him of most of his speech and partly inhibited movement on his right-hand side. Swedish composers have since written several left-hand piano pieces especially for him to play.

Since his stroke, he has published a short book of 'autobiographical chapters', *Memories Look at Me* (1993) and a new collection, *The Sad Gondola* (1996), both included in Robin Fulton's translation of his Bloodaxe *New Collected Poems* (1997). In 2004 he published *The Great Enigma*, a slim volume containing five short poems and a group of 45 even smaller haiku-type poems. These were added to the *New Collected Poems* to form Tranströmer's first collected edition to appear in the States, published by New Directions in 2006 under the title *The Great Enigma: New and Collected Poems*.

Tranströmer has also translated other poets into Swedish, including Robert Bly and Hungary's János Pilinszky. In 1990 he received the Neustadt International Prize for Literature. His other awards include the Bonner Award for Poetry, Germany's Petrarch Prize, the Bellman Prize, the Swedish Academy's Nordic Prize, and the August Prize. In 1997 the city of Västerås established a special Tranströmer Prize.

From foreword to Tranströmer's *New Collected Poems* (Bloodaxe Books, 1997) and *The Great Enigma: New and Collected Poems* (New Directions, USA, 2006).

The Movement of Tranströmer's Poetry
by ROBIN FULTON

Over 40 years ago Transtromer wrote a poem called 'Morning Birds', which concludes with the idea of the poem growing while the poet shrinks:

> It grows, it takes my place.
> It pushes me aside.
> It throws me out of the nest.
> The poem is ready.

He could hardly have envisaged then how aptly such an idea would come to describe his career. On the one hand we have the private person who was born in Stockholm in 1931 and grew up there, who spent many years in Västerås working as a psychologist, and has now returned to Stockholm to live in the very area in which he spent his youth. The same private person has spent as much time as possible out in the Stockholm archipelago, on Runmarö, an island rich in family associations and a place which, I suspect, he feels is his real home. [...]

On the other hand we have the poet whose gathered work takes up very little space on the bookshelf: if run-on, his poems now would fill scarcely 200 pages. As he says in the memoir of his grammar-school days, he became 'well-known for deficient productivity'. For over half a century, however, as they slowly accumulated, his poems have attracted special attention in his native Sweden and in the course of at least three decades they have caught the interest of an extraordinary range of readers throughout the world via translations into all major and many minor languages. [...]

The way in which much or even most of Tranströmer's poetry describes, or allows for, or tries to come to terms with the powerful elements of our lives which we cannot consciously control or even satisfactorily define suggests, rightly, that there is a profoundly religious aspect to his response to the world and therefore in his poetry. In a largely secular country like Sweden such a writer may well be asked about religion in rather a blunt or naive manner (as if 'Do you believe in God?' were the same kind of question as 'Do you vote Social Democrat?') and Tranströmer has always replied to such questions cautiously. The following (from the Gunnar Harding interview already mentioned) is a characteristic response to the comment that reviewers sometimes refer to him as a mystic and sometimes as a religious poet:

> Very pretentious words, mystic and so on. Naturally I feel reserved about their use, but you could at least say that I respond to reality in such a way that I look on existence as a great mystery and that at times, at certain moments, this mystery carries a strong charge, so that it does have a religious character, and it is often in such a context that I write. So these poems are all the time pointing towards a greater context, one that is incomprehensible to our normal everyday reason. Although it begins in something very concrete

This movement towards a larger context is very important and it reflects Transtömer's distrust of over-simple formulations, slogans and rhetorical gestures as short-cuts that can obscure and mislead.

SOME RESPONSES TO TOMAS TRANSTRÖMER'S WORK:

'Transtömer is a vivid evoker of both landscapes and cityscapes... The writer, he says, is "at the same time eagle and mole", looking down or looking up from the vantage point best suited to catching life before it disappears. Transtömer is especially good at memorable moments of panic, uncertainty, displacement, from which the speaker can recover but which remind him of darknesses and worlds no one would want to inhabit for long' – EDWIN MORGAN, *Northwords*.

'One of the most outstanding poets of our time...Transtömer has succeeded in achieving a synthesis between the modern and the traditional, between art and life. He has been able to breathe life into some of the most uninspiring realities of modern existence... He has worked for more than thirty years as a practising psychologist, helping people, giving them something of his remarkable integrity and strength, and achieving a depth of vision into our human condition that he is able to express in his poems' – JAAN KAPLINSKI.

TOMAS TRANSTRÖMER
Response to *Uj Iras*

The following was published – in Hungarian – in the Hungarian magazine *Uj Iras*, in 1977. The magazine had asked me, and some other European poets, to describe my own poetry and give my view of the situation for modern poetry in general, 'its possibilities'.

Nearly ten years ago, the editor of an anthology managed to squeeze the following self-characterisation out of me:

> My poems are meeting-places. Their intent is to make a sudden connection between aspects of reality that conventional languages and outlooks ordinarily keep apart. Large and small details of the landscape meet, divided cultures and people. How together in a work of art, Nature meets Industry etc. What looks at first like a confrontation turns out to be a connection.
>
> Conventional languages and outlooks are necessary when it's a question of *handling* the world, of reaching clearly-defined and concrete goals. But we know from experience that these fall short in the most important moments of life. If we permit them to dominate us wholly, we are on the road to the breakdown of contact, to destruction. I view poetry as a counter move against that sort of development. Poems are active meditations, they want to wake us up, not put us to sleep.'

That was ten years ago but it can still stand as an answer to *Uj Iras*'s question about how I view my work. Now to the question of how I view contemporary poetry, 'its situation, its possibilities'. In my civilisation it's customary to describe poetry as discarded, almost moribund, an all-too exclusive art form, without power to break through. And the poets try to push themselves upon the world of the mass media, try to get a few crumbs of attention. I think it's time to emphasise that poetry – in spite of all the bad poets and bad headers – starts from an advantageous position. A piece of paper, some words: it's simple and practical. It gives independence. Poetry requires no heavy, vulnerable apparatus that has to be lugged around, it isn't dependent on temperamental performers, dictatorial directors, bright producers with irresistible ideas. No big money is at stake. A poem doesn't come in one copy that somebody buys and locks up in a storeroom waiting for its market value to go up; it can't be stolen from a museum and become currency in the buying and selling of narcotics, or get burned up by a vandal.

When I started writing, at 16, I had a couple of like-minded school friends. Sometimes, when the lessons seemed more than usually trying we would pass notes to each other between our desks – poems and aphorisms, which would come back with the more or less enthusiastic comments of the recipient. What an impression those scribbings would make! *There* is the fundamental situation of poetry. The lesson of official life goes rumbling on. We send inspired notes to one another.

Article translated by Judith Moffett and published in *Ironwood 13*, vol.7 no.1, *Tranströmer: A Special Issue*.

TOMAS TRANSTRÖMER
Neustadt Laureate's Words of Acceptance

Let me sketch two ways of looking at a poem. You can perceive a poem as an expression of the life of the language itself, something organically grown out of the very language in which it is written – in my case, Swedish. A poem written by the Swedish language through me. Impossible to carry over into another language.

Another, and contrary, view is this: the poem as it is presented is a manifestation of another, invisible poem, written in a language behind the common languages. Thus, even the original version is a translation. A transfer into English or Malayalam is merely the invisible poem's new attempt to come into being. The important thing is what happens between the text and the reader. Does a really committed reader ask if the written version he reads is the original or a translation?

I never asked that question when I, in my teenage years, learned to read poetry – and to write it (both things happened at the same time). As a two-year-old child in a polyglot environment experiences the different tongues as one single language, I perceived, during the first enthusiastic poetry years, all poetry as Swedish. Eliot, Trakl, Éluard – they were all Swedish writers, as they appeared in priceless, imperfect, translations.

Theoretically we can, to some extent justly, look at poetry translation as an absurdity. But in practice we must believe in poetry translation, if we want to believe in World Literature.

From speech given at Norman, Oklahoma, on 12 June 1990, reprinted from *World Literature Today*, 64:4 (Autumn 1990).

'Exorcism' *(opposite)* is from Tomas Tranströmer's *Memories Look at Me* (1993), and is reprinted – along with all the poems which follow – from *New Collected Poems*, translated by Robin Fulton (Bloodaxe Books, 1997). Dates in brackets show when each poem was first published in book form in Sweden.

Exorcism

During the winter when I was 15 I was afflicted by a severe form of anxiety. I was trapped by a searchlight which radiated not light but darkness. I was caught each afternoon as twilight fell and not released from that terrible grip until next day dawned. I slept very little, I sat up in bed, usually with a thick book before me. I read several thick books in that period but I can't say I really read them for they left no trace in my memory. The books were a pretext for leaving the light on.

It began in late autumn. One evening I'd gone to the cinema and seen *Squandered Days*, a film about an alcoholic. He finishes in a state of delirium – a harrowing sequence which today I would perhaps find rather childish. But not then.

As I lay down to sleep I reran the film in my mind's eye, as one does after being at the cinema.

Suddenly the atmosphere in the room was tense with dread. Something took total possession of me. Suddenly my body started shaking, especially my legs. I was a clockwork toy which had been wound up and now rattled and jumped helplessly. The cramps were quite beyond the control of my will, I had never experienced anything like this. I screamed for help and Mother came through. Gradually the cramps ebbed out. And did not return. But my dread intensified and from dusk to dawn would not leave me alone. The feeling that dominated my nights was the terror which Fritz Lang came near to catching in certain scenes of *Dr Mabuse's Testament*, especially the opening scene – a print works where someone hides while the machines and everything else vibrate. I recognised myself in this immediately, although my nights were quieter.

The most important element in my existence was *Illness*. The world was a vast hospital. I saw before me human beings deformed in body and in soul. The light burned and tried to hold off the terrible faces but sometimes I would doze off, my eyelids would close, and the terrible faces would suddenly be closing in on me.

It all happened in silence, yet within the silence voices were endlessly busy. The wallpaper pattern made faces. Now and then the silence would be broken by a ticking in the walls. Produced by what? By whom? By me? The walls crackled because my sick thoughts wanted them to. So much the worse... Was I insane? Almost.

I was afraid of drifting into madness but in general I did not feel threatened by any kind of illness – it was scarcely a case of hypochondria – but it was rather the total power of illness that aroused terror. As in a film where an innocuous apartment interior changes its character entirely when ominous music is heard, I now experienced the outer world quite differently because it included my awareness of that domination wielded by sickness. A few years previously I had wanted to be an explorer. Now I had pushed my way into an unknown country where I had never wanted to be. I had discovered an evil power. Or rather, the evil power had discovered me.

I read recently about some teenagers who lost all their joy in living because they became obsessed with the idea that AIDS had taken over the world. They would have understood me.

Mother had witnessed the cramps I suffered that evening in late autumn as my crisis began. But after that she had to be held outside it all. Everyone had to be excluded, what was going on was just too terrible to be talked about. I was surrounded by ghosts. I myself was a ghost. A ghost that walked to school every morning and sat through the lessons without revealing its secret. School had become a breathing space, my dread wasn't the same there. It was my private life that was haunted. Everything was upside down.

At that time I was sceptical towards all forms of religion and I certainly said no prayers. If the crisis had arisen a few years later I would have been able to experience it as a revelation, something that would rouse me, like Siddhartha's four encounters (with an old person, with a sick person, with a corpse, and with a begging monk). I would have managed to feel a little more sympathy for and a little less dread of the deformed and the sick who invaded my nocturnal consciousness. But then, caught in my dread, religiously coloured explanations were not available to me. No prayers, but attempts at exorcism by way of music. It was during that period I began to hammer at the piano in earnest.

And all the time I was growing. At the beginning of that autumn term I was one of the smallest in the class, but by its end I was one of the tallest. As if the dread I lived in were a kind of fertiliser helping the plant to shoot up.

Winter moved towards its end and the days lengthened. Now, miraculously, the darkness in my own life withdrew. It happened gradually and I was slow in realising fully what was happening. One spring evening I discovered that all my terrors were now marginal. I sat with some friends philosophising and smoking cigars. It was time to walk home through the pale spring night and I had no feeling at all of terrors waiting for me at home.

Still, it is something I have taken part in. Possibly my most important experience. But it came to an end. I thought it was Inferno but it was Purgatory.

Prelude

Waking up is a parachute jump from dreams.
Free of the suffocating turbulence the traveller
sinks towards the green zone of morning.
Things flare up. From the viewpoint of the quivering lark
he is aware of the huge root-systems of the trees,
their swaying underground lamps. But above ground
there's greenery – a tropical flood of it – with
lifted arms, listening
to the beat of an invisible pump. And he
sinks towards summer, is lowered
in its dazzling crater, down
through shafts of green damp ages
trembling under the sun's turbine. Then it's checked,
this straight-down journey through the moment, and the wings spread
to the osprey's repose above rushing waters.
The bronze-age trumpet's
outlawed note
hovers above the bottomless depths.

In day's first hours consciousness can grasp the world
as the hand grips a sun-warmed stone.
The traveller is standing under the tree. After
the crash through death's turbulence, shall
a great light unfold above his head?

[1954]

Secrets on the Way

Daylight struck the face of a man who slept.
His dream was more vivid
but he did not awake.

Darkness struck the face of a man who walked
among the others in the sun's strong
impatient rays.

It was suddenly dark, like a downpour.

I stood in a room that contained every moment –
a butterfly museum.

And the sun still as strong as before.
Us impatient brushes were painting the world.

[1958]

Tracks

2 A.M.: moonlight. The train has stopped
out in the middle of the plain. Far away, points of light in a town,
flickering coldly at the horizon.

As when a man has gone into a dream so deep
he'll never remember having been there
when he comes back to his room.

As when someone has gone into an illness so deep
everything his days were becomes a few flickering points, a swarm,
cold and tiny at the horizon.

The train is standing quite still.
2 A.M.: bright moonlight, few stars.

[1958]

The Journey's Formulae
(from the Balkans, 1955)

1

A murmur of voices behind the ploughman.
He doesn't look round. The empty fields.
A murmur of voices behind the ploughman.
One by one the shadows break loose
and plunge into the summer sky's abyss.

2

Four oxen come, under the sky.
Nothing proud about them. And the dust thick
as wool. The insects' pens scrape.

A swirl of horses, lean as in
grey allegories of the plague.
Nothing gentle about them. And the sun raves.

3

The stable-smelling village with thin dogs.
The party official in the market square
in the stable-smelling village with white houses.

His heaven accompanies him: it is high
and narrow like inside a minaret.
The wing-trailing village on the hillside.

4

An old house has shot itself in the forehead.
Two boys kick a ball in the twilight.
A swarm of rapid echoes. – Suddenly, starlight.

5

On the road in the long darkness. My wristwatch
gleams obstinately with time's imprisoned insect.

The quiet in the crowded compartment is dense.
In the darkness the meadows stream past.

But the writer is halfway into his image, there
he travels, at the same time eagle and mole.

[1958]

Allegro

I play Haydn after a black day
and feel a simple warmth in my hands.

The keys are willing. Soft hammers strike.
The resonance green, lively and calm.

The music says freedom exists
and someone doesn't pay the emperor tax.

I push down my hands in my Haydnpockets
and imitate a person looking on the world calmly.

I hoist the Haydnflag – it signifies:
'We don't give in. But want peace.'

The music is a glass-house on the slope
where the stones fly, the stones roll.

And the stones roll right through
but each pane stays whole.

[1962]

The Half-Finished Heaven

Despondency breaks off its course.
Anguish breaks off its course.
The vulture breaks off its flight.

The eager light streams out,
even the ghosts take a draught.

And our paintings see daylight,
our red beasts of the ice-age studio;

Everything begins to look around.
We walk in the sun in hundreds.

Each man is a half-open door
leading to a room for everyone.

The endless ground under us.

The water is shining among the trees.

The lake is a window into the earth.

[1962]

Nocturne

I drive through a village at night, the houses rise up
in the glare of my headlights – they're awake, want to drink.

Houses, barns, signs, abandoned vehicles – it's now
they clothe themselves in Life. – The people are sleeping:

some can sleep peacefully, others have drawn features
as if training hard for eternity.
They don't dare let go though their sleep is heavy.
They rest like lowered crossing-barriers when the mystery draws past.

Outside the village the road goes far among the forest trees.
And the trees the trees keeping silence in concord with each other.
They have a theatrical colour, like firelight.
How distinct each leaf! They follow me right home.

I lie down to sleep, I see strange pictures
and signs scribbling themselves behind my eyelids
on the wall of the dark. Into the slit between wakefulness and dream
a large letter tries to push itself in vain.

[1962]

Winter's Formulae

1

I fell asleep in my bed
and woke up under the keel.

At four o'clock in the morning
when life's clean picked bones
coldly associate with each other.

I fell asleep among the swallows
and woke up among the eagles.

2

In the lamplight the ice on the road
is gleaming like lard.

This is not Africa.
This is not Europe.
This is nowhere other than 'here'.

And that which was 'I'
is only a word
in the December dark's mouth.

3

The institute's pavilions
displayed in the dark
shine like TV screens.

A hidden tuning-fork
in the great cold
sends out its tone.

I stand under the starry sky
and feel the world creep
in and out of my coat
as in an ant-hill.

4

Three dark oaks sticking out of the snow.
So gross, but nimble-fingered.
Out of their giant bottles
the greenery will bubble in spring.

5

The bus crawls through the winter evening.
It glimmers like a ship in the spruce forest
where the road is a narrow deep dead canal.

Few passengers: some old and some very young.
If it stopped and quenched the lights
the world would be deleted.

[1966]

Alone

I

One evening in February I came near to dying here.
The car skidded sideways on the ice, out
on the wrong side of the road. The approaching cars –
their lights – closed in.

My name, my girls, my job
broke free and were left silently behind

88

further and further away. I was anonymous
like a boy in a playground surrounded by enemies.

The approaching traffic had huge lights.
They shone on me while I pulled at the wheel
in a transparent terror that floated like egg white.
The seconds grew – there was space in them –
they grew as big as hospital buildings.

You could almost pause
and breathe out for a while
before being crushed.

Then something caught: a helping grain of sand
or a wonderful gust of wind. The car broke free
and scuttled smartly right over the road.
A post shot up and cracked – a sharp clang – it
flew away in the darkness.

Then – stillness. I sat back in my seat-belt
and saw someone coming through the whirling snow
to see what had become of me.

II

I have been walking for a long time
on the frozen Östergötland fields.
I have not seen a single person.

In other parts of the world
there are people who are born, live and die
in a perpetual crowd.

To be always visible – to live
in a swarm of eyes –
a special expression must develop.
Face coated with clay.

The murmuring rises and falls
while they divide up among themselves
the sky, the shadows, the sand grains.

I must be alone
ten minutes in the morning
and ten minutes in the evening.

– Without a programme.

Everyone is queuing at everyone's door.

Many.

One.

[1966]

Sketch in October

The tug is freckled with rust. What's it doing here so far inland?
It's a heavy extinguished lamp in the cold.
But the trees have wild colours: signals to the other shore.
As if someone wanted to be fetched.

On my way home I see mushrooms sprouting through the grass.
They are the fingers, stretching for help, of someone
who has for long sobbed alone in the darkness down there.
We are the earth's.

[1973]

Looking through the Ground

The white sun is soaking through the smog.
The light drips, gropes its way down

to my deep-down eyes that are resting
deep under the city looking up

seeing the city from below: streets, foundations –
like aerial photos of a city in war

the wrong way round – a mole photo:
silent squares in sombre colours,

The decisions are taken there. No telling
bones of the dead from bones of the living.

The sunlight's volume is turned up,
it floods into flight-cabins and peapods.

[1973]

from **Baltics**

VI

Grandmother's story before it's forgotten: her parents die young,
father first. When the widow knows the disease will take her too
she walks from house to house, sails from island to island
with her daughter. 'Who can take Maria?' A strange house
on the other side of the bay takes her. There they have the means.
But that didn't make them good. The mask of piety cracks.
Maria's childhood ends too early, she's an unpaid servant
in perpetual coldness. Year after year. Perpetual seasickness
during the long stints of rowing, solemn terror
at table, the looks, the pike-skin scrunching
in her mouth: be grateful, be grateful.
                                        She never looked back
but because of that she could see what was new
and catch hold of it.
Out of encirclement.

I remember her. I would press close to her
and at the moment of death (the moment of crossing?) she sent out a
        thought
so that I – a five year old – understood what happened
half an hour before they rang.

Her I remember. But on the next brown photo
the unknown man –
dated by his clothes to the middle of last century.
A man around thirty: the vigorous eyebrows,
the face looking straight into my eyes
and whispering: 'here I am'.
But who 'I' am
there's no one any more who remembers. No one.

91

TB? Isolation?

Once coming up from the sea
on the stony slope steaming with grass he stopped
and felt the black bandage on his eyes.

Here, behind dense thickets – is it the island's oldest house?
The low, two-centuries-old fisherman's hut, log-cabin style, with
heavy coarse grey timbers.
And the modern brass padlock has clicked it all together and shines
like the ring in the nose of an old bull
who refuses to get up.
So much wood crouching. On the roof the ancient tiles which have
slipped downways and crossways over each other
(the original pattern deranged over the years by the rotation of the
earth)
it reminds me of something… I was there… wait: it's the old Jewish
cemetery in Prague
where the dead live more packed than they were in life, the stones
packed packed.
So much love encircled! The tiles with their lichen-script in an
unknown tongue
are the stones in the ghetto cemetery of the archipelago folk, the
stones raised and tumbled. –
The hovel is lit up
with all those who were driven by a certain wave, by a certain wind
right out here to their fates.

[1974]

From March 1979

Weary of all who come with words, words but no language
I make my way to the snow-covered island.
The untamed has no words.
The unwritten pages spread out on every side!
I come upon the tracks of deer's hooves in the snow.
Language but no words.

[1983]

Fire-Jottings

Throughout the dismal months my life sparkled alive only when
        I made love with you.
As the firefly ignites and fades out, ignite? and fades out, – in
        glimpses we can trace its flight
in the dark among the olive trees.

Throughout the dismal months the soul lay shrunken, lifeless,
but the body went straight to you.
The night sky bellowed.
Stealthily we milked the cosmos and survived.

[1983]

Dream Seminar

Four thousand million on earth.
They all sleep, they all dream.
Faces throng, and bodies, in each dream –
the dreamt-of people are more numerous
than us. But take no space...
You doze off at the theatre perhaps,
in mid-play your eyelids sink.
A fleeting double-exposure: the stage
before you out-manoeuvred by a dream.
Then no more stage, it's you.
The theatre in the honest depths!
The mystery of the overworked director!
Perpetual memorising of new plays...
A bedroom. Night.
The darkened sky is flowing through the room.
The book that someone fell asleep from lies
still open
sprawling wounded at the edge of the bed.
The sleeper's eyes are moving,
they're following the text without letters
in another book –

illuminated, old-fashioned, swift.
A dizzying commedia inscribed
within the eyelids' monastery walls.
A unique copy. Here, this very moment.
In the morning, wiped out.
The mystery of the great waste!
Annihilation. As when suspicious men
in uniforms stop the tourist –
open his camera, unwind the film
and let the daylight kill the pictures:
thus dreams are blackened by the light of day.
Annihilated or just invisible?
There is a kind of out-of-sight dreaming
that never stops. Light for other eyes.
A zone where creeping thoughts learn to walk.
Faces and forms regrouped.
We're moving on a street, among people
in blazing sun.
But just as many – maybe more –
we don't see
are also there in dark buildings
high on both sides.
Sometimes one of them comes to the window
and glances down on us.

[1983]

Leaflet

The silent rage scribbles on the wall inwards.
Fruit trees in blossom, the cuckoo calls.
It's spring's narcosis. But the silent rage
paints its slogans backwards in the garages.

We see all and nothing, but straight as periscopes
wielded by the underground's shy crew.
It's the war of the minutes. The blazing sun
stands above the hospital, suffering's parking-place.

We living nails hammered down in society!
One day we shall loosen from everything.
We shall feel death's air under our wings
and become milder and wilder than here.

[1989]

April and Silence

Spring lies desolate.
The velvet-dark ditch
crawls by my side
without reflections.

The only thing that shines
is yellow flowers.

I am carried in my shadow
like a violin
in its black case.

The only thing I want to say
glitters out of reach
like the silver
in a pawnbroker's.

[1996]

A Page of the Night-Book

I stepped ashore one May night
in the cool moonshine
where grass and flowers were grey
but the scent green.

I glided up the slope
in the colour-blind night
while white stones
signalled to the moon.

A period of time
a few minutes long
fifty-eight years wide.

And behind me
beyond the lead-shimmering waters
was the other shore
and those who ruled.

People with a future
instead of a face.

[1996]

Silence

Walk past, they are buried...
A cloud glides across the sun's disk.

Starvation is a tall building
that moves by night

in the bedroom a lift-shaft opens
it's a dark rod pointing to the inner domains.

Flowers in the ditch. Fanfare and silence.
Walk past, they are buried...

The table-silver survives in big shoals
deep down where the Atlantic is black.

[1996]